101
WAYS TO SAY
THANK YOU

NOTES OF
GRATITUDE FOR
ALL OCCASIONS

KELLY BROWNE

With a foreword by Dorothea Johnson
Founder of the Protocol School of Washington®

STERLING

New York / London
www.sterlingpublishing.com

To my wonderful husband and our precious children—
I am eternally grateful . . .

A portion of the author's royalties have been donated
to St. Jude Children's Research Hospital.

STERLING and the distinctive Sterling logo are registered trademarks of Sterling
Publishing Co., Inc.

Library of Congress Cataloging-in-Publication Data
Browne, Kelly.
   101 ways to say thank you : notes of gratitude for all occasions / by Kelly Browne ;
with a foreword by Dorothea Johnson.
      p. cm.
   Includes index.
   ISBN-13: 978-1-4027-4702-1
   ISBN-10: 1-4027-4702-0
   1. Thank-you notes. I. Title. II. Title: One hundred and one ways to say thank you.
III. Title: One hundred one ways to say thank you.

BJ2115.T45B76 2007
395.4--dc22   2007030253

   10 9 8 7 6

Published by Sterling Publishing Co., Inc.
387 Park Avenue South, New York, NY 10016
© 2008 by Kelly Browne
Distributed in Canada by Sterling Publishing
c/o Canadian Manda Group, 165 Dufferin Street
Toronto, Ontario, Canada M6K 3H6
Distributed in the United Kingdom by GMC Distribution Services
Castle Place, 166 High Street, Lewes, East Sussex, England BN7 1XU
Distributed in Australia by Capricorn Link (Australia) Pty. Ltd.
P.O. Box 704, Windsor, NSW 2756, Australia

Book design and layout: Rachel Maloney

Manufactured in the United States of America
All rights reserved

Sterling ISBN-13: 978-1-4027-4702-1
        ISBN-10: 1-4027-4702-0

For information about custom editions, special sales, premium and corporate
purchases, please contact Sterling Special Sales.
Department at 800-805-5489 or specialsales@sterlingpublishing.com.

Foreword

Hail the handwritten note! It has been around for hundreds of years, and we will not witness its demise simply because some of its everyday functions have been replaced by e-mail and voice mail. Of course, it's a given that e-mail and telephones are most efficient for staying in touch and handling daily communications, but when it comes to a cut above, paper and pen rule.

Kelly Browne takes a modern, common-sense—albeit elegant—approach to note writing. Though highly practical, this book's lively text makes it a joy to peruse. Ms. Browne's guidelines will encourage you to pick up your pen and express yourself in ways that messages delivered via telephone or e-mail simply can't convey.

If the people of the world become a little more thoughtful about showing gratitude by writing notes, it will be in no small measure thanks to the efforts of Kelly Browne.

Dorothea Johnson
Founder of The Protocol School of Washington®

Acknowledgments

I'd like to thank the people who made this book possible.

Linda Konner, I am tremendously grateful to you for your insight, vision, and integrity. Jo Fagan, Hannah Reich, and everyone at Sterling Publishing, thank you from the bottom of my heart for publishing this book. Megan Kuntze, Robert Murray, and Crane & Company, thank you for promoting the importance of etiquette and gratitude, and for supplying exquisite paper worldwide for three hundred years. Dorothea Johnson, you are indeed the epitome of class and style. I sincerely thank you for your heartfelt support and advice, and for always maintaining high standards of protocol. Kimberly Wileman, I am indebted to you for our lifelong friendship. Christine, Jack, and Gretchen, it is an honor to be your sister. To my parents, Richard and Peggy Learman, my love for you both is never ending. Mom, thank you for teaching me how to say thank you and for instilling the spirit of charity in my heart. Dad, your kindness and generosity are unsurpassed. Thank you for always being proud of me and encouraging me to find the story. Greta and Ava, my little treasures, thank you for giving me the reason to write this book. Sam, thank you for patiently teaching me how to be the mother I am today. My husband, Aric, I thank God every day for the gift of sharing my life with you. And finally, St. Jude, thank you for listening.

Peace begins with a smile.

—MOTHER TERESA, HUMANITARIAN AND NOBEL LAUREATE

CONTENTS

Gratitude is the most exquisite form of courtesy.

—Jacques Maritain, French philosopher

Introduction

Every young woman knows that sending the classic handwritten thank-you note is as essential as her little black dress. Now more than ever before, people are embracing the time-honored tradition of remembering the thoughtfulness of a friend, relative, or business associate with a formal note of thanks. Yes, we're all busy, but in this world of instant electronic communication, nothing stands out more or lets people know how much you appreciate their act of kindness than a thank-you note.

If embracing your inner regal nature isn't enough or if your mother's constant reminders have not provided sufficient motivation, consider that *not* acknowledging someone for the gift of generosity can be hurtful. Remember your reputation before you decide your life is too hectic to say thank you. Studies have shown that when someone says thank you, it creates a chain-reaction of kindness that in turn promotes a cycle of gratitude. It shouldn't be a mystery why so many philosophers and religions embrace gratitude as a valuable state of well-being. Imagine the positive effect we could each have if we made showing our appreciation a part of our daily practice.

Starting today, commit to making a habit of thanking the people you encounter daily for the little things they do for you, for example, the doorman who rushes into the rain to find you a cab, or your assistant who works late to help you look good, or even an inspirational teacher who has made a difference in your life. You'll be amazed how much people appreciate being acknowledged for their acts of kindness. The truth is, in one small second, something magical happens that can affect both of you. So when you assume you don't have the ability to promote world peace, think again. The magic words are "please" and "thank you!"

With many thanks to my mother's insistence, I learned that a meaningful thank-you note really does make a difference, not only in the life of the person you are thanking, but also in your own. My mother was right. Being truly thankful has changed my life for the better. This book is designed to help people everywhere reap the same benefits I have—by learning to cultivate gratitude and by sharing that appreciation through thank-you notes that can really make a difference.

You'll find my personal guide to the basics in "Thank-You Notes 101" as well as sample thank-you notes for everything from wedding gifts and birthday presents to those intangible gifts of support that make life so much easier during difficult times. I hope my notes will inspire you when you write your own. You'll also find a variety of "Quips" and "Tips" from "Grateful Sages" who knew the power of showing appreciation, as well as quick-and-easy checklists to help you say thank you with grace and style.

It is my hope that this book will encourage you to spend a little more time counting your blessings and letting people know how much their thoughtfulness and generosity have meant to you, and that by putting your gratitude and thankfulness into action you make our world a better place.

A thousand thank-yous . . .

Kelly Browne

I've learned that people will forget what you said, people will forget what you did, but people will never forget how you made them feel.

—MAYA ANGELOU, AMERICAN POET AND NOVELIST

Chapter 1
Thank-You Notes 101:
Getting Back to Basics

Just as you are slipping into those fabulous strappy heels and heading for the door, something catches your eye. In the corner of the room sits the open box with the pink cashmere sweater Aunt Greta sent you weeks ago. Of course you meant to thank her but somehow it just never happened. If you don't do it now, chances are you'll forget about it again, and the last thing you want is for anyone to believe you are ungrateful. Rather than come up with a list of excuses, just be the lady you truly are and write that thank-you note as graciously as possible. But, where do you start?

January 16, 2008

Dear Aunt Greta,

Thank you so much for the sweater. Hope you are doing well.

Love,

Ava

Not so good. Try again…

January 16, 2008

Dear Aunt Greta,

Thank you so much for the gorgeous pink sweater. It looks lovely with my new skirt and is perfect for my interview next week. You always find such special treasures! Thank you for thinking of me, and I hope you are well.

Love,

Ava

Not only is the second version much better in sentiment, but more important, when Aunt Greta opens her mailbox and reads your thank-you note she will feel the magic sparkle of gratitude come back to her for her generosity to you.

Writing the Classic Thank-You Note

It's actually easy to write a thank-you note because the format is always the same: the date, salutation, your thank-you message, the closing, and your signature. Break it down like this:

1. WRITE THE DATE.
   January 16, 2008

2. WRITE THE SALUTATION.
   Dear (put person's name here),

   ❋ "Dear" is the most popular salutation to use, but you can also use "Dearest" for a loved one or your own term of endearment, depending on the situation.

   ❋ Remember to use a comma following the salutation and addressee's name for all handwritten notes, social or casual.

❊ If you're writing a thank-you note to a couple, you can write the note to one of them and mention the other in the text of the note or you can address it to both of them.

❊ Use "Mr. and Mrs." for formal notes and use first names for more intimate or casual relationships.

3. WRITE THE CONTENT OF YOUR THANK-YOU NOTE.
Thank the person for the gift as genuinely and graciously as you can. Try to add something extra like, "I look forward to seeing you soon," or "I hope you're doing well," or "My mother sends her love," or even the famous "Let's do lunch."

GRATEFUL SAGE TIP
If you have trouble putting it all together, write it out first on a piece of scrap paper, then copy it neatly.

4. WRITE THE CLOSING.
For formal and business notes

Sincerely,   Very sincerely,
Sincerely yours,   Very sincerely yours,

SIX DO'S FOR ELEGANT NOTES

1. Do handwrite your note neatly, without mistakes, on good-quality stationery using blue or black ink.

2. Do use glowing superlatives and energetic adjectives like fabulous, amazing, delightful, and extraordinary. Be creative. Really think about the moment you opened the gift and how you felt, and then tell the giver about it. Be expansive and passionate and convey your emotion.

3. Do mention in your thank-you note how you plan to use the gift. This shows that the gift was well chosen, and that's one of the best ways to say thank you.

4. Do add a compliment such as, "You have wonderful taste," or "How do you always know just what to get for me?" or "You are such a thoughtful and kind person, and I'm so grateful to have you in my life." People like to know they're appreciated.

5. Do keep your note to a paragraph or two in length. Remember, it's a note, not a letter. You can make it longer if you want to, but it's not expected.

6. Do make each note sound special and unique to the person, situation, and gift. Thank-you notes should never feel generic.

GRATEFUL SAGE TIP
Consider not sending gifts or doing favors for people when you feel they expect it and if they fail to thank you!

Glowing Superlatives and Energetic Adjectives
Try some of these words to add a little excitement to your notes!

amazing	incredible
astonishing	iridescent
astounding	lively
attractive	lovely
awe-inspiring	luminous
beautiful	marvelous
beyond belief	miraculous
bright	multicolored
brilliant	out of this world
colorful	outstanding
dazzling	radiant
excellent	remarkable
exceptional	rich
extraordinary	shimmering
fabulous	shining
fine-looking	sparkling
generous	spectacular
gleaming	splendid
glistening	startling
glowing	striking
good-looking	stunning
gorgeous	surprising
handsome	unbelievable
hard to believe	vibrant
incandescent	vivid
inconceivable	wonderful

For Thank-You Notes of Love and Friendship

Affectionately,	With affection,
Fondly,	With warmest regards,
Love,	Your friend,
Love always,	Yours,
Truly yours,	Yours truly,
Warmly,	

For Thank-You Notes for Special Gifts and Favors

Gratefully,	Gratefully yours,

For Thank-You Notes to Clergy and Statesmen

Faithfully yours,	Sincerely yours,
Respectfully,	Yours faithfully,
Respectfully yours,	

For General Thank-Yous

Best regards,	My best wishes for your
Best wishes,	quick recovery,
Best wishes for your health and happiness,	

5. ADD YOUR SIGNATURE.

Your first name

or

Your first and last name.

* Most commonly, people sign their first name for personal relationships and their full name for formal ones.

* Make sure your signature is legible. Often signatures become a bunch of circles or a squiggly line, and the recipient of your note is left baffled as to who you might be.

* If you write your thank-you note electronically and then print it, you must handwrite your name.

* If your signature is illegible, you might want to use personalized stationery.

Your note should look like this on the page:

January 16, 2007

Dear Grandma Esther,

Thank you for the very generous check you sent. I desperately need to get a new printer for my computer, and now I can buy one, thanks to you! Now all my papers for school will be on time. I truly appreciate that you are always thinking of me. You are a very special person

Love,

Ava

THE STATIONERY WARDROBE

A "stationery wardrobe" consists of versatile stationery that you can readily use for any occasion and that gives you the opportunity to reflect your unique personality. Your choice of paper, color, size, and weight makes a statement not only about you, but about what you think of your recipient. Your stationery can be engraved, thermographed (raised printing), or flat-printed. Your choice of stationery should always suit the occasion. Whether your needs are social or business, a stationery wardrobe is a valuable tool. Typically a wardrobe will contain:

❋ Correspondence cards (4¼″ × 6½″): The most versatile stationery for writing short notes, thank-yous, and invitations; only the front may be used. These can be printed with your monogram, crest, or name and are usually a heavier paper weight.

❋ Informals (5¼″ × 3½″): While their name might sound confusing, "informals" are actually formal notes. Folded in half and often referred to as "fold-overs," informals can be printed with your name or monogram on the front. For a level of high formality, choose paper colors ecru or white with your proper social name in black engraving. For example,
MRS. RICHARD MELDRUM LEARMAN.

❋ Single sheet stationery: Printed with your name and address at the top, the choice of these papers is up to you and depends on the length and formality of your letters. If a second sheet is needed, a blank one should be used. Lighter in weight, they can fit through a printer, if necessary.

❋ Note sheets (6⅜″ × 8½″): Perfect for social use.

❋ Monarch or executive stationery (7¼″ × 10½″): These sheets are used for both social letters and personal business letters.

✿ Standard letter sheets (8½″ × 11″): Most frequently used for business letters.

✿ Envelopes: Keep in mind that stationery wardrobes are often created to make it possible to use one size envelope for several different sizes of paper. Envelopes should include a return address, but including your name is optional.

✿ Calling cards: Varying in size and similar to a business card, calling cards are for new acquaintances and include your personal contact information, such as your name, phone number, e-mail address, and home address. You can simply use your name and phone number if you wish.

Start with your most essential pieces—one for your thank-you notes and one for writing letters.

GRATEFUL SAGE TIP

While engraving is the most elegant and expensive way to print your stationery at the outset, once the die cast has been cut it can be used again and again—making it less expensive in the long run.

Social and Savvy Stationery for the Perfect Thank-You

Traditionally, the appropriate formal social stationery to use for thank-you notes is of good quality and is white or ecru in color. However, pastel colors have also become acceptable and popular.

❋ The most formal of social stationery is the traditional fold-over note called the "informal." These can be plain or personalized with your monogram, crest, or name. When folded, they measure approximately 5¼″ × 3½″. They can also be used for invitations and short notes.

❋ Correspondence cards with your name or monogram printed across the top, with a small design, or embellished with a border are also popular. They are typically a heavier card stock and measure 4¼″ × 6½″ in size. Only the front side of the card is used.

❋ Boxes of good-quality fold-over notes that have "Thank You" or a small design printed on the cover of the flap are readily available at most stationery stores. The inside is blank for your note.

❋ Single and boxed blank cards with a beautiful picture on the front make great thank-yous. Many museums sell them in their gift shops.

❋ Cards with a preprinted inscription of thanks are also available. These are fine in casual situations where you write a personal thank-you note inside the card. It is *not* acceptable just to sign your name. Why? Because someone took the time to do something special for you and it is important for you to thank the person properly.

❋ Affordable personalized stationery wardrobes are available printed with your name and address. These can make your thank-you note writing and social correspondence easier.

THE DO'S AND DON'TS OF USING HONORIFICS

1. Do remember that an honorific refers to titles that show respect or honor, such as: Mr., Mrs., Miss, and Ms.

2. Do include the appropriate honorific in the formal and business thank-you note as well as on the envelope.

3. Do use "Miss" if you are addressing a single woman in a formal or social note.

4. Do use "Ms." for professional women, divorced women resuming their maiden name, or when you are uncertain of a woman's marital status.

5. Don't use an honorific for yourself when signing your name to your thank-you note.

6. Do use "Mr. and Mrs." when addressing a married couple followed by the husband's first and last name: "Mr. and Mrs. Russel Fish."

7. Do use "Mrs." when formally addressing a married woman followed by her husband's name: "Mrs. Richard Meldrum Learman."

8. Do include "Mrs." for a divorced woman retaining her married name, followed by her first, maiden, and married names: "Mrs. Margaret Kerrigan Barry."

9. Do use "Doctor" as either the full word or the abbreviation "Dr." when addressing a male doctor and his wife: "Dr. and Mrs. Irving Iscoe." In addressing a husband and wife where she is the doctor, both full names can appear on the same line or hers on a separate line above his.

10. Do check the appropriate title to use when addressing your note to a statesman, academic, or a member of the clergy or royalty.

Computer-Ready Stationery

If you decide to create your thank-you note on the computer,
you have a vast selection of stationery to choose from. It is very
easy to print different sizes of paper on your printer. Use the
"page setup" menu when creating your new document and
adjust the page size to that of your paper and envelope. If you
are creating a fold-over note, for example, you will need to click
on "margins" (within the "page setup" menu) to adjust the left-
and right-hand margins and also to adjust the top margin so
your text will appear below the fold. Make sure you do a test
run on inexpensive paper before using your best stationery.

There is a wide variety of paper to choose from, ranging
from the highest quality to the inexpensive. As long as it isn't
too thick or too small for your printer, high-end preprinted
personalized stationery will work and will look lovely.
Watermarked, 100 percent cotton paper, which is available in
varying weights, always looks more elegant than copy paper.
Copy paper should never be used for thank-you notes.

And the Envelope, Please…

That little envelope is just as important as your thank-you note, so please don't cast it off as insignificant. Remember, it's the very first thing the recipient sees when your note arrives, and you want to make a favorable impression immediately. Your thank-you note is a reflection of you!

The addressee's name should begin at the center of the envelope with the street address directly under it. The next line is the city, state, and zip code. Be sure to include your return address in the upper left corner of the envelope.

The front of your envelope should look like this:

Your Name
1234 Street Avenue
Town, ST 90000-1234

Mrs. Gift Giver
4321 Street Avenue
Anytown, ST 80000-4321

Insert your thank-you note into the envelope with the folded side up and the front of the note facing toward you, so the flap of the envelope closes down over the front of the note.

SIX SIMPLE DO'S AND DON'TS FOR
THE ELEGANT ENVELOPE

1. Do make sure you double-check the address before you write it on the front of the envelope.

2. Do handwrite your envelope if your note is handwritten (which is always best).

3. Don't send a typed or computer-printed thank-you note with a hand-addressed envelope. Whatever you choose, they should match.

4. Don't use clear, stick-on address labels; they look impersonal. Putting the envelope through your printer is a much better choice than using a label. The traditional route is always handwritten.

5. Do include the last four digits of the nine-number zip code for United States addresses, for example, 91000-1234. It will get there faster! If you don't know the full zip code, check it on the Internet at www.usps.com.

6. Do check out the variety of stamps available at your local post office or online. There are so many beautiful stamps to choose from, and they can help make your note that much more special.

Handwritten Notes Versus Computer-Generated Notes

Traditionally, thank-you notes are handwritten neatly on good-quality stationery, have no mistakes, and are in blue or black ink. This is by far the most socially acceptable manner in which to offer a thank-you note. It is personal, gracious, and thoughtful. In today's electronic world the handwritten note is even more valued. However, many of us feel embarrassed by our handwriting, which can make writing a thank-you note a very intimidating and awkward situation—especially when we want to look graceful. So which is worse, not sending a thank-you note or typing one? The answer is obvious. There is absolutely no reason you cannot type your thank-you note or create one on your computer if you are faced with this situation. In fact, there are several advantages if you choose to go the computer-generated route. For example, you can use the spell-check on your word processing program and catch any mistakes you may have missed. Your note is neat, legible, and often better thought out, because you can delete what you wrote and start over! We are often committed to what we have started in handwritten notes because we don't want to waste the paper or write it all over again.

GRATEFUL SAGE TIP

Look for a basic script font that looks like handwriting, but stay away from the styles that are too ornate and difficult to read.

∞

The E-Mailed Thank-You

While e-mail is the least preferred way in which to send a formal thank-you note, it is a wonderful alternative in business, casual, and personal relationships. For example, if your best friend gave you her favorite recipe or sent you an article on a subject of interest to you, it would be perfectly fine to send an e-mail thank-you. On the other hand, you should never use it to send thank-you notes for wedding presents or baby gifts.

Always use your best judgment. If you aren't sure about sending an e-mail thank-you note, don't. Just remember, handwritten notes are always greatly appreciated.

The Golden Rules for Timely Thank-You Success

1. Do send your thank-you note immediately, so you won't forget.
2. Do remember to send a thank-you note within two weeks of receiving a gift.
3. Do acknowledge wedding gifts within three months of their receipt.
4. Do keep in mind that a phone call never counts as a thank-you! A note must be sent after the call.

Damage Control for Late Thank-You Notes

At some point, you will be faced with having to send a late thank-you note. No matter how hard you try, you can't do everything in that extra five minutes you thought you had. Regardless of how late you are, you should send a thank-you note. Yes, the person may be hurt or offended that you did not show your appreciation in a timely manner, but a sincere note can soften the situation.

First, how late are you? If you are within days or a week or two of the reasonable time limit, don't worry about it. Send your note and don't bother to mention it. If, however, you are sending out a thank-you note for a wedding gift you received seven months earlier—be honest. You can explain briefly that you were late in sending it out: "While filling the gorgeous vase you gave me for our wedding with beautiful red roses, it suddenly occurred to me that I never sent you a thank-you note! Please forgive me." Then continue with your note.

You can always call the person to acknowledge the gift and then send a note, too. Sometimes this can help smooth a situation over, especially if you share a personal moment, for example, describing something funny that happened on your honeymoon or how you felt when you heard your baby cry for the first time.

I awoke this morning with devout thanksgiving for my friends, the old and the new.

—RALPH WALDO EMERSON, TRANSCENDENTALIST WRITER

Chapter 2
SOIREES AND SOCIAL GATHERINGS

Thanks for Having Me

As every gracious young woman knows, cultivating an active social calendar is an important element in creating a successful and fulfilling adult life. Dinner parties, charity events, dances, and social gatherings not only keep you engaged in the rich tapestry of life but often lead to new and exciting relationships and opportunities you never would have encountered if you had not been invited. Without the occasional soiree, gala, and reception to look forward to, when would you ever have an excuse to put on that sparkly gown and those completely impractical strappy heels? So the next time you step out in style, let your hosts know what a great time you had, by thanking them for inviting you. A grateful guest is a frequent guest.

Writing the Social Thank-You Note

1. Remember that all the same basic rules apply to the social or formal thank-you note, so make sure you refer to the previous chapter, "Thank-You Notes 101."
2. The use of honorifics is important here, too. If you're sending a thank-you note to your best friend's parents for inviting you to her debutante ball make sure you use "Mr. and Mrs."
3. Pay attention to your closing as well. A formal honorific requires an elegant closing. "Sincerely" or "Sincerely yours" are more appropriate choices than such casual closings as "With affection."

4. The fold-over informal note or social stationery in white or ecru is always the best choice. Use black or blue ink when you write the note.

The Formal Social Envelope

For formal thank-you notes, the socially correct envelope format is slightly different. The first option is to stagger the lines, with the recipient's name centered on the envelope, followed by the street address underneath and slightly to the right of center, followed by the city, state, and zip code underneath and slightly farther to the right of the address. There should be no abbreviations; everything should be spelled out.

The front of the formal envelope should look like this:
Mrs. Herman Horowitz
1234 Street Place
Town, State 80000-4321

Or it can be centered like this:
Mrs. Herman Horowitz
1234 Street Place
Town, State 80000-4321

The return address should be printed on the back flap of the envelope or written there in your best penmanship. While you can include your formal name, the preferred style is to use only your address. The back flap of the envelope should look like this:
9000 Avenue Road
Big City, State 10000-1234

More Golden Rules for Social Thank-You Success

1. Do remember to call your hostess the day after a dinner party you attended the night before, then follow up with a thank-you note.

2. Always send a thank-you note within two weeks of attending an event or benefit if you were invited as someone's guest. A thank-you note would not be expected if you were invited to attend an event and purchased your own ticket.

3. Avoid delays. Make sure you always have appropriate stationery on hand to use when necessary.

QUIPS FROM GRATEFUL SAGES THROUGH THE AGES
∽

For it is in giving that we receive.

—St. Francis of Assisi

To educate yourself for the feeling of gratitude means to take nothing for granted, but to always seek out and value the kind that will stand behind the action. Nothing that is done for you is a matter of course. Everything originates in a will for the good, which is directed at you. Train yourself never to put off the word or action for the expression of gratitude.

—Dr. Albert Schweitzer, Nobel laureate

Gratitude is not only the greatest virtue, but the parent of all others.

—Cicero, Roman philosopher

Keep a gratitude journal. Every night, list five things that you are grateful for. What it will begin to do is change your attitude about your day, and your life.

—Oprah Winfrey, talk-show host

If you knew what I know about the power of giving, you would not let a single meal pass without sharing it in some way.

—Buddha, enlightened teacher

Pay It Forward

BE AN AMBASSADOR OF GOODWILL

Jacqueline Kennedy Onassis had an incredibly full social calendar, but she presented herself to the world as an ambassador of goodwill with unforgettable grace and dignity. My mother, too, is an example for us all. She has been volunteering her time for as long as I can remember—not just standing for countless hours making and serving casseroles at church functions—but even organizing a charity ball to help runaway children. From spearheading paper drives to tennis tournaments, she still finds the time to create and donate gorgeous gift baskets to honor the World War II heroes of the Mighty Eighth Air Force. As I watch her in admiration, I see the utter joy and appreciation in the faces of people whose lives she has directly influenced by her kindness. This has truly changed my life.

Perhaps you're thinking you don't have time to work out at the gym, much less volunteer at a soup kitchen. There are things you can do every day to share your appreciation with the world. Donate your old clothes to a battered women's shelter, put your trash in the garbage can, recycle, help someone less fortunate than yourself, make a phone call to help a friend get a job, or give food to a homeless person. Even speaking kindly and respectfully to others is an important contribution. Be an ambassador of goodwill and people will remember you.

Carry out a random act of kindness with no expectation of reward, safe in the knowledge that one day someone might do the same for you.

—Diana, Princess of Wales

Thanks for Having Me—Sample Notes

It is essential to send a thank-you note for each event you have been invited to as a guest. Whether it be a dinner, a weekend at someone's home, or a charity event, a note of thanks must be sent. On the following pages are some sample thank-you notes you can copy, fill in, or just use for inspiration as you write your own.

Thanks for the Dinner or Dinner Party

Dear _____,

I just wanted to thank you again for the wonderful dinner at your lovely home last evening. I so appreciate your attention to every detail and the love you put into everything you do. Please know I will remember this special night for a long time to come.

Sincerely yours,

_____

Thanks for the Fabulous Gala

Dear Mrs. Learman,

The Angel's Flight Christmas Gala was simply spectacular. It was truly as if we were dancing through a sparkling winter wonderland. Thank you for including me in your elegant affair, which has definitely spoiled me forever. I wish you my heartfelt congratulations on the success of this event and offer my sincere appreciation to you for inviting me as your guest.

Most sincerely,

Isabel Posada

Thank You for the Invitation—Regret

Dear _____,

Thank you so much for the invitation to your party. Unfortunately, I am already committed for that evening and will be unable to attend. I appreciate your thinking of me and know it will be a great success. Please keep me on your list for the next time.

Sincerely yours,

_____

Thank You for Inviting Me to the Mardi Gras Masquerade

Dear Mr. and Mrs. Jessee,

There is simply nothing more exciting than your annual Mardi Gras Masquerade Ball. Just wearing a black-feathered mask and feeling mysterious for the evening was really a thrill. The music so electrified the crowd that everyone danced past midnight, including me! Dear David and Jane are still recovering from their attempts at the tango. Thank you for a magical, star-filled night.

Sincerely yours,

Frances Gibbs

GRATEFUL SAGE TIP

Stationery and boxed thank-you notes make a perfect hostess gift.

∽≫⌒

Thank You for the Inspiring Museum Exhibit

Dear Mr. Iscoe,

I am well aware that the Van Gogh exhibit at the Metropolitan Museum of Art was a difficult ticket to get. Needless to say, I was simply thrilled when you called and invited me to attend the opening gala. Of course, seeing works of art by a legendary master was truly an experience I will never forget. Thank you for such a wonderful treat and the opportunity to enjoy this historic night.

Sincerely yours,

Greta Browne

Thanks for Inviting Me to the Reception

Dear Mr. Ambassador,

What a pleasure it was to meet you last evening at the Irish Embassy reception for Senator Webster. I am a huge supporter of the work that you have done in third-world countries, and I hope our lawmakers look to your ideas for peace. If there is anything I can do to support your mission, please let me know. Thank you for including me in this unforgettable night.

Respectfully yours,

Gretchen Learman

Thank You, the Tea Party was Terrific

Dear Mrs. Raymond,

The Teddy Bear Tea for St. Jude's Hospital was truly an event I will never forget. I so appreciated your inviting me to attend and giving me the opportunity to see firsthand the work that is being done for these deserving children. Please include me on the guest list for next year. Thank you again for such a special day.

Sincerely,

Joan Cunningham

Thank You for the Weekend Away

Dear Mr. and Mrs. Angel,

My weekend at your home in the Hamptons was simply magical. I can still smell the delicious seaside BBQ we had Saturday night and taste that fabulous chocolate cake. How did the two of you become such incredible gourmet chefs? Please know I appreciated that you made me feel so welcome in every way. I look forward to seeing you both again soon.

Sincerely yours,

Samara

No one has ever become poor by giving.

—ANNE FRANK, DUTCH WRITER

Chapter 3
PERSONAL MILESTONES AND SPECIAL MOMENTS

Thanks for the Wonderful Memories

Whether you're graduating, celebrating a birthday, moving into a new home, marking a personal achievement, attending your first ball, or embarking on your next global tour, the good wishes—and, of course, the many thoughtful gifts from family and friends—make those remarkable moments in life truly special, creating memories that will last a lifetime. So the next time you reach a personal milestone, take a moment to let people know how much their love and generosity mean to you.

GRATEFUL SAGE TIPS

If you don't know what to give the person who seems to have everything, think about making a financial contribution in that person's name to a favorite charity.

Even if you thanked someone enthusiastically when you opened the gift, you must still send a thank-you note.

Make your note personal and conversational; write it as if you were speaking with the person who gave you the gift.

QUIPS FROM GRACIOUS AND SPECIAL SAGES THROUGH THE AGES

ॐ

The more you praise and celebrate your life, the more there is in life to celebrate.

—OPRAH WINFREY, TALK-SHOW HOST

If the only prayer you ever say in your whole life is "thank you," that would suffice.

—MEISTER ECKHART, GERMAN PHILOSOPHER

Forget injuries, never forget kindnesses.

—CONFUCIUS, CHINESE PHILOSOPHER

The wisest men follow their own direction.

—EURIPIDES, CLASSICAL GREEK PLAYWRIGHT

May you always have work for your hands to do.
May your pockets hold always a coin or two.
May the sun shine bright on your windowpane.
May the rainbow be certain to follow each rain.
May the hand of a friend always be near you.
And may God fill your heart with gladness to cheer you.

—IRISH BLESSING

Sparkling Birthstones

These gems make fabulous birthday gifts!

January	Garnet
February	Amethyst
March	Aquamarine, bloodstone
April	Diamond (great for all occasions!)
May	Emerald
June	Pearl, moonstone, alexandrite
July	Ruby
August	Peridot, sardonyx
September	Sapphire
October	Opal, tourmaline
November	Topaz, citrine
December	Turquoise, zircon

Thanks for the Wonderful Memories—Sample Notes

Here are some sample notes to help you say thanks for the memories with elegance and impact.

Thank You for My Birthday Gift

Dear _____,

How very thoughtful of you to think of me on my birthday. I just love the (gift) and want you to know that every time I (wear it, see it, use it) I think of you. Thank you for all your generosity. I look forward to seeing you soon.

With all my love,

_____

Thank You, Mom and Dad, for My New Wheels or Other Spectacular Gift

Dear Mom and Dad,

There are simply no words to express how much I appreciate
your helping me buy a (car/something fabulous)! Never did I
imagine that   (on my birthday/graduation/just because)
my dream would come true. I know you have both worked hard
to give me this awesome gift and in return I want you to know
that I will continue to focus on my (schoolwork/career/other
efforts). Thank you for believing in me and having confidence
in my ability to make good decisions.

With all my love,

_____

Thank You for the Best Friend Spa Birthday

Dear Maria,

I couldn't wait to be 21. Then when the time came, I realized
the one person I wanted to share this special birthday with was
my best friend. Having a glorious spa day at the Camelback
Inn was beyond belief! I loved our leisurely manicures, stone
massages, and yogurt parfaits by the desert pool. Thank you
for making this day something I will treasure for a lifetime.

Lots of love,

Inez

Bon Voyage!

Dear Ivette,

It was so incredibly sweet of you to throw me a bon voyage party! I am really looking forward to going to Paris, and you know, I will miss you desperately. I love the pink mini blow-dryer and the all-in-one electrical appliance conversion kit almost as much as the Champagne and tiny Eiffel Tower on the cake. Now I have more room to pack an extra outfit or two. Thank you for making it très magnifique! Au revoir, mon amie!

Merci,

Mademoiselle Sophie

Thanks for Coming to My Debutante Ball

Dear Mrs. Mente,

What an honor it was to have you attend my Debutante Ball over the Thanksgiving weekend. You are someone I deeply admire for all the selfless charity work you have done throughout your life. I love the pearl earrings and want you to know that every time I wear them, I will think of you. Thank you for sharing this unforgettable evening with me.

Sincerely,

Gloria Landman

Thanks, Professor, from a Grateful Graduate

Dear Professor Krasilovsky,

I can't believe the moment I have worked so hard for over the past four years has finally arrived. While I am excited to graduate and move into the next chapter of my life, it is also bittersweet. You have had a huge impact on my life, have broadened my horizons, and have allowed me to reach farther than I ever dreamed I could. I'll never forget you. Thank you, Professor, for making a difference in my life.

Most sincerely,

Alexis

Thanks for Coming to My Graduation

Dear _____,

I want you to know how much it meant to me to have you at my graduation. Looking out into the audience and seeing you cheering as I received my diploma was a moment I will never forget. Thank you for sharing this special day and always supporting me when I panicked over every test and paper. You were right: one page at a time, one test at a time. Thank you for believing in me.

Sincerely yours,

_____

Thanks for the Fabulous Graduation Gift— Wish You Were Here!

Dear _____,

How very generous of you to send me a check for my graduation from _____. Although I wished you were here, I knew that all your good wishes were with me. Please know that I so appreciate the check and I plan on (putting it to good use/using it to pay off my student loans/getting a new computer/buying a suit for my first job interview). Let's celebrate the next time we're together. Thank you so very much.

With affection,

_____

GRATEFUL SAGE TIPS

Remember, even if you send out or receive a graduation announcement card, a gift isn't required in return.

The next time someone asks you for gift ideas, request personalized stationery; then send that person a thank-you note on it!

Thanks, Mom and Dad, for College

Dear Mom and Dad,

I am sure this thank-you note seems unexpected, but it is no less sincere. I know I may have seemed ungrateful over these past four years and I apologize for that. I simply never thought I'd make it though all those final exams and research papers, but I did, thanks to both of you. I can see now that you have given me so much more than I ever dreamed possible. Please know this moment of graduating has made an indelible mark on my life. Thank you for giving me a future and insisting that I finish school. Now I can achieve anything.

With all my love,

_____

Thank You for Warming My New Home with
Your Love and Good Wishes

Dear Warren and Tony,

There was no way in the world I could have ever moved into my new apartment without both of you! Thank you for helping me carry all those boxes up so many flights of stairs. If you are free next week I would love to thank you both properly and invite you back for my mother's special apricot chicken and chocolate chip cake.

Gratefully yours,

Gabriela

We make a living by what we get. We make a life by what we give.

—SIR WINSTON CHURCHILL, ENGLISH STATESMAN

Chapter 4
CLIMBING THE LADDER
OF SUCCESS

Thanks for the Opportunity

The ability to write a gracious and memorable thank-you note has advantages that extend far beyond the social world and can actually make the difference in getting your dream job or creating your golden opportunity. Writing a thank-you note following a job interview not only shows the interviewer that you have good, professional manners, it also helps you stand out from the crowd of other candidates. Even if you don't get the job, sending a good-natured thank-you note reiterating your interest can turn rejection into a new possibility for success, should things change. Like everything else, business involves maintaining good relationships with the people you meet along the way and making sure they realize how grateful and appreciative you are for any help they can offer. So the next time you're planning to take a step up the ladder of success, remember to look behind you and thank the people who gave you a break or put in a good word for you. They will appreciate it, and you will too when you land the job of your dreams!

GRATEFUL SAGE TIP
If you don't personally thank someone who helped you, chances are that person won't help you again.

When to Send the Business Thank-You

1. Immediately following a job interview.
2. Send a note to any person who spoke on your behalf, referred you for a position, or wrote a letter of recommendation for you.
3. If you don't get the job, send a thank-you note reiterating your interest should a position become available later.
4. If company circumstances change and the job is no longer available, thank your contacts for taking the time to speak with you and ask if they'll pass along your résumé.
5. Send thank-you notes when people do something thoughtful for you such as referring business, taking you to lunch or dinner, sending you a gift, or giving you tickets to a game or event.
6. Business owners should take the time to thank their customers for their continued loyalty.
7. If you're leaving your current position it is gracious to include a personal note of thanks along with your resignation letter.

GRATEFUL SAGE TIP

A traditional way to thank a client or friend in a small but polite way is to take the person out for a cup of coffee. Coffee gift cards are an affordable alternative and an excellent idea to include with your thank-you note. Think creatively!

༄

Format of a Typed Business Thank-You Note

A handwritten thank-you note is always elegant, but there are companies that don't regard business interviews as social occasions. A handwritten powder-pink thank-you note following an interview for a high-security position in the military or the government would be unprofessional. So use your best judgment and do what you feel is appropriate for the situation.

The business thank-you note opens the door for further communication and gives you the ability to add one more point to your interview. Use this opportunity as your final selling tool. There's no need to restate your résumé, but do use this note for any additional ideas you might have or to add something you forgot to say in the interview. How well you write this note will also indicate what kind of representative you will make for their company and your level of desire to be there. The way you represent yourself will reflect how you will represent them. More important, you are demonstrating that you are not only smart but also a woman with excellent values and social graces.

A professional letter, the business thank-you note includes proper spacing, the date, and company contact information as well as your personal contact information.

It should look like this:

April 26, 2008 (date at the top of the page)

(four line spaces between the date and person's name)

Ms. Kimberly Wileman

Galla Worldwide

4321 West 57th Street

New York, NY 10019

(two line spaces between the last address line and your salutation)

Dear Ms. Wileman: (use a colon here instead of a comma)

(one line space here)

I wanted to take a moment to thank you for meeting with me this afternoon. I am well aware of the pressure and excitement that accompany working at Fashion Week, *and I appreciate the generous time you took to look at my work. Although I am a recent graduate of design school, I have spent many hours interning with several noted designers and I know how much hard work it takes to create a successful line.*

(one line space between paragraphs.)

While I am aware that this week is hectic for you and possibly not the best time to think about new job candidates, I want to let you know once again that it would be my pleasure to join your team. I am attaching a color copy of one of my designs for your reference.

(one line space)

I will follow up with you next week.

(one line space)

Sincerely,

(four line spaces)

Vivian Barone
youremailaddress@internetmail.com
Your phone number
Your address

GRATEFUL SAGE TIP

For security, some women today are eliminating their home address from their résumé and using only their phone number and e-mail address. This is a good thing to remember if you post your résumé with a headhunter or on the Internet.

Ten Things Every Grateful Interviewee Should Know

1. Research the company before the interview so you know enough about it to appear interested and ask informed questions.
2. Dress appropriately and always arrive early.
3. Shake your interviewer's hand firmly when you meet her, look her in the eye, and thank her for the opportunity for the interview. Make sure you say thank you again when you leave.
4. Get your interviewer's business card. Then you are sure all your information is correct.
5. Get her e-mail address. It's an easy way to follow up later.
6. Don't forget to thank the assistant, too. Assistants are truly the portal guardians, and being kind and gracious to them really helps to ensure your access.
7. Send your thank-you note immediately. By doing so, you show the kind of mannerly executive or employee you will make for the company.
8. Look around your interviewer's office and note something unique in the surroundings. It will help you make a personal connection in your thank-you note and will show you were paying attention. This is perfect if you are interviewing for marketing, sales, or ad agency jobs and will provide an opportunity to demonstrate your creative expertise. For example, if there is a fish tank on your interviewer's desk, choose a card with fish on it. Remember, handwrite the entire note, don't just sign it.
9. Your interviewer will look at your educational background. In today's competitive job market, having a degree is vital to your success. If you want that dream job you've wished for your whole life, you have to work hard to get it.
10. If you need experience to get the job you want, consider doing volunteer work or working as an intern. These are easy ways for you to start a résumé even when you are still in high school or college.

The Successful Business Note Checklist

❋ Do send your thank-you note immediately and no later than two days following the job interview. An immediate follow-up to your meeting shows you would make a conscientious and productive employee, executive, consultant, or vendor.

❋ Do keep your note sincere and professional while limiting it to one page.

❋ Do use fonts that are business-appropriate.

❋ Don't use any other ink color but black or blue.

❋ Do keep your closing professional. "Sincerely" is always an excellent choice.

❋ Do handwrite your signature.

❋ Do proofread your letter. Always read it out loud and use the spell-check option in your word processing program. You can lose a job simply because you were sloppy.

❋ Do reiterate your desire for the position, clarify any uncertainties the interviewer might have expressed, and show your strengths.

❋ Do indicate you'll follow up, and when. Ask for the sale!

❋ Don't make the mistake of forgetting to change the interviewer's name in the address and "Dear" sections if you are sending out more than one thank-you note that's been created on your computer.

The Business Stationery Checklist

❃ Do use paper that is a higher quality than regular white copy paper.

❃ Standard business size 8½" × 11" sheets are available in watermarked, 100 percent cotton paper in ecru or white. Stay away from colors.

❃ Monarch sheets or executive sheets are smaller and available in 7¼" × 10½" size. These are perfect for the personal business note and fit easily through a printer if necessary.

❃ The business correspondence card size is 4½" × 6½" and is a heavier card stock. They are used for occasions that are professional but a bit more personal.

❃ Do order customized letterhead with your name and address or create your own on the computer.

❃ Always use a matching envelope that includes your return address.

GRATEFUL SAGE TIP
Office supply stores carry Crane & Company letter-size business paper for your thank-you notes and also for your cover letter and résumé, too. Visit www.crane.com to view the selections.

൞

Virtual Gratitude: The Fundamentals of Thank-You Note Netiquette

Many corporations today prefer using e-mail for the majority of their business. It makes sense then, that many companies readily accept this form of thank-you note for interviews, meetings, or business lunches and dinners because it is efficient, cost effective, professional, and instantaneous. Whether to send an e-mail thank-you note is really a matter of discretion. If you are interviewing to work at a law firm that is bogged down by paper, you may want to cut through those stacks, bypass the assistant, and send an e-mail straight to your interviewer. Always use your best judgment.

✳ The advantage of e-mail is that it is immediately received by your interviewer.

✳ Remember that e-mail is never private.

✳ An e-mail thank-you to your interviewer must look professional, be well thought out, and avoid the use of Internet slang.

✳ Don't run home and send your e-mailed thank-you note. You just left. Wait a few hours. The objective is to remind them of you.

✳ Keep in mind that your thank-you note could be caught by a spam filter and never arrive!

✳ Maintain a professional e-mail address. You don't want to lose your job opportunity because your interviewer feels your e-mail address is inappropriate. Using your name, initials, or a combination thereof is always a good option. If your choice isn't available, try using a number at the end of your name, for example: JillianFish6@internet.com.

The format of an e-mailed thank-you note is really a blend of the handwritten and the business notes. Because the addressee's e-mail is already included, there's no need to rewrite it in the body of the message unless you want to. Typically, the e-mail thank-you includes your salutation, followed by the person's name, your thank-you message, the closing, and your name, followed by your contact information. It should look like this:

To: Frank.Learman@consolidated.com
From: EstherMeldrum@internet.net
Date: 2-15-2008
Subject: Thank you
Message:

Dear Mr. Learman:
I just wanted to follow up and let you know how much I appreciated meeting with you today. It would be such an honor for me to work at Consolidated and participate in the development of cutting-edge aerospace technology. Should a position become open in your Research and Development department, please let me know.

Thank you again for taking the time to meet with me.
Sincerely,
Esther Meldrum
(415) 555-1212—mobile
(415) 555-1313—home
450 Center Drive
San Francisco, CA 90005-1234

GRATEFUL SAGE TIP
When in doubt about which type of thank-you to use, choose the typed note because it is the most common format in the business world.

QUIPS FROM PRESIDENTIAL SAGES THROUGH THE AGES

In writing or speaking, give to every person his due title according to his degree and custom of the place.

—GEORGE WASHINGTON, *RULES OF CIVILITY & DECENT BEHAVIOR IN COMPANY AND CONVERSATION*

Common sense and consideration should be the basis of etiquette and good manners.

—JOHN QUINCY ADAMS

As we express our gratitude, we must never forget that the highest appreciation is not to utter words, but to live by them.

—JOHN FITZGERALD KENNEDY

Gratitude is a way to a deeper wisdom. Look for the deeper wisdom; believe me, there's a great hunger for it. And here you're in luck. As Americans, you have a special claim to it.

—RONALD REAGAN

Pay It Forward

VOLUNTEERING FOR SUCCESS

Volunteer work is critical to your success and has an enormous positive effect on your résumé. It presents you not only as someone who is willing to give back to your community without expecting anything in return, but it also sets you apart from the other job candidates. My mother encouraged my participation in National Charity League, a mother-daughter debutante program designed to promote volunteer service in the community. As part of the program, I worked for years with the Crippled Children Society, now known as AbilityFirst. I stuffed envelopes, collected money, and worked with children to earn my volunteer hours. In college, my sorority, Delta Delta Delta, continued this spirit of giving back. I didn't know it at the time, but it changed me forever. I learned to be patient, compassionate, thankful, and nonjudgmental. I began to look at the world in a different way. After a while I realized that the things that were really important to me didn't have a price tag on them. During a job interview, the person who interviewed me was impressed that while I was in high school and college I had spent a significant amount of time helping other people. I was hired on the spot.

Volunteering isn't about giving up your summer or even your whole life and joining the Peace Corps. Helping to organize or participating in an act of charity not only puts volunteer hours on your résumé, it makes you feel good. Such experiences will definitely change your life and also give you needed experience in your field. Even business owners benefit when they participate in local and national campaigns to raise awareness for a cause. Their business gets exposure, customers feel they're contributing, and as a result repeat business is likely. The bottom line is that everybody wins.

The Collegiate Thank-You

The choice of where you go to school can have a profound
effect on the rest of your life. Here, too, the thank-you note can
really make a difference, so be sure to send one within two
days of your college interviews. Remember, thousands of
people are applying for those few spots. It's possible that you
could secure a spot based on the fact that you followed up and
demonstrated responsibility, civility, and determination.
Sending a thank-you note gives you a great opportunity to
reiterate how much you want to receive an acceptance letter.
It's also important to write thank-you notes to all the people
who wrote letters of recommendation for you. If they take time
to help you, they deserve to be thanked.

Faxing Your Thank-You Note

Of course you can fax your thank-you note, but it certainly
isn't the preferred method of delivery. Keep in mind that most
companies use the fax machine frequently, and your note could
be forgotten or lost along with the jammed paper. The last thing
you want is for your gracious effort to end up on the floor.

THE THANK-YOU THESAURUS
Power Words that Move Mountains

ability
accomplished
aficionado
authority
brilliant
capable
clout
committed
competent
connoisseur
consultant
creative
cultured
dedicated
devoted
educated
enthusiastic
equipped
experienced
expert
familiar
fit

gifted
influence
knowledgeable
power
practiced
professional
proficient
qualified
refined
skilled
skillful
sophisticated
specialist
stylish
talented
technically savvy
veteran
well-informed
well-read
well-traveled
wiz

GRATEFUL SAGE TIP

Use a thesaurus; there are many ways to say the same thing, only better! Most word processing programs will have a built-in thesaurus.

The History of "Ms."

According to Dorothea Johnson, founder of The Protocol School of Washington®, "Ms." is the correct honorific for a woman in the business arena regardless of what she chooses to call herself in her private life. Revived by twentieth-century feminists, "Ms." has been around since at least the seventeenth century as an abbreviation for the honorific "Mistress," which applied to both married and unmarried women, and from which both "Miss" and "Mrs." derive.

GRATEFUL SAGE TIP

If you receive a gift that you feel is inappropriate or has a monetary value that is above company policy, return it with a thank-you note saying you can't accept it.

├

Business Owners: Thank You for Your Continued Loyalty

Whether your business is enormous or consists of a small group of clients, the fact remains that your customers appreciate being thanked for their continued loyalty. With our increasing reliance on technology, the personal touch can make all the difference in the growth and success of your business. Thanking your clients—however large or small the business they do—can promote a deeper sense of loyalty to you, increase business, and help secure referrals. Equally important is thanking the people who work for you. You will benefit when you thank them for their work, and dedication. After all, they are contributing to your success. It's also important for you to model the kind of behavior you would like your staff to project. If you give the gift of gratitude, you will receive it in return.

In this arena, there are limitless ways to show your appreciation:

- ❋ Provide your employees with thank-you cards to send out to all their best customers.

❊ Send thank-yous via e-mail if your company is Internet based.

❊ Send your customers gift cards or coupons to your store for "customer appreciation" day.

❊ Send out gift baskets, bottles of wine, or gift cards to restaurants or stores for the holidays or "just because."

❊ Cater lunch for your employees to show how much you appreciate their time and energy, or create a new policy such as birthdays off—with pay!

❊ Throw a lunch or dinner and publicly recognize a good quality of each of your associates. They will appreciate it.

❊ Put your company logo on overnight bags, sweatshirts, polo shirts, or just about anything you can think of, and give these items to your best customers and your employees. It's also a wonderful way to promote your business.

Thanks for the Opportunity—Sample Notes
Customize any of these thank-you notes to suit your personal needs!

Thank You for the Business Interview

Dear Mrs._____:

I just wanted to follow up on my interview with you today and let you know how much I appreciated your taking the time to meet with me. During our conversation you mentioned several projects (name of company) is currently working on. It would be my pleasure to put some ideas together to come in and present to you. I look forward to hearing from you at your earliest convenience.

Sincerely,

Thank You for Looking at My Project/Script/Proposal

Dear Mr. _____:

Per our conversation, please find enclosed (project name, script title, proposal) for your consideration. I appreciate your taking the time to read it and I look forward to hearing your thoughts.

If you have any questions, please don't hesitate to contact me.

Sincerely,

_____

Dear Ms._____:

Thank you for returning my material to me and including your notes and ideas. It isn't often that someone takes the time to go the extra mile, and I appreciate all of your effort to help me. I'd love to keep the door open to send you my (projects/ scripts/proposals) in the future. A thousand thanks.

Best regards,

_____

Thank You for Speaking on My Behalf

Dear Mr. _____:

It meant the world to me that you took the time to speak on my behalf. Please know that not only do I appreciate your interrupting your busy day to help me, but I value the kind words you said about me. Thank you.

Sincerely,

_____

Thank You for Letting Us Look at Your Project/Script/Proposal

Dear Ms. _____:

We really enjoyed reading (name of your project/script/proposal),
but unfortunately it isn't something that we are in a position to
pursue at this time. Please know we appreciate your thinking of us,
and we wish you every success in finding a home for it.

Best regards,

_____

Dear Mr._____:

Thank you so much for contacting us regarding your
(project/script/proposal) for our consideration. Unfortunately,
given the large number of submissions we receive on a daily
basis, we are unable to accept unsolicited material. Please
review our policies and procedures, which may be found on
our website at www.nameofyourcompany.net.

Best regards,

_____

GRATEFUL SAGE TIP
"Best regards" is the most common closing to use if
you are pursing a career in the entertainment industry.

Thank You for the Interview—Maybe Next Time

Dear Mr._____:

Thank you for updating me on the _____ position at (business name). Please know that if anything should change or if a new position becomes available, I would be interested in returning to meet with you. Thank you again for your time and consideration.

Sincerely,

_____

Thank You for Your Loyalty—Customer

Dear Mrs._____:

You have been a loyal customer of ours for the past (number of months/years), and to show our appreciation we'd like to present you with the enclosed (gift card/coupon) to be used on (Customer Appreciation Day/your next purchase/at your convenience). Thank you for being a part of the (name of company) family.

Sincerely,

(Name of president/owner)

Dear _____:

Thank you for the confidence you have placed in us. As a company dedicated to excellence in customer satisfaction, please let us know if we can be of further assistance.

We appreciate your trust.

Sincerely yours,

_____

Thank You for Your Charitable Donation

Dear Mr. _____:

Thank you for your charitable donation to (name of charity). It is because of generous gifts from good-hearted people like you that we are able to make a significant difference in the lives of so many (children/people/seniors). Your contribution will be used to (briefly mention use). From the bottom of our hearts, we thank you.

Sincerely,

_____

Thank You for the Business Gift

Dear Ms. _____:

When your gift arrived at the office today, everyone cheered and congregated in the conference room. I have never seen a group of dignified people tear through chocolate chip cookies (or another baked item) in such a short amount of time. Thank you for the delicious gift.

Sincerely,

_____

Thank You for the Business Lunch or Dinner

Dear Mr. _____:

What a pleasure it was to meet with you over lunch this afternoon. I think we accomplished a great deal and I look forward to working together. If you have any further questions or concerns, please let me know. Thank you again for the excellent meal and conversation.

Sincerely,

_____

Thanks for Helping Make the Company a Success

Dear _____:

As a small way of saying thank you for your hard work and continued loyalty at (name of business), please find enclosed a gift card to be used at the store, restaurant, or hotel of your choice. We recognize your dedication and we truly appreciate valuable associates like you. Thank you.

Most sincerely,

_____

GRATEFUL SAGE TIP

Include your business card with your note. Some businesses have their cards made into magnets that make them easier to find and refer to.

⁂

Thank You for the Letter of Recommendation

Dear Professor_____:

I am so extremely grateful to you for writing a letter of recommendation on my behalf. You are someone I hold in high regard and view with a tremendous amount of respect. Please know how much I appreciate your endorsement. I hope to use it not only for graduate school applications but in the business world as well. Thank you.

Most sincerely,

_____

Thank You for the Offer, But . . .

Dear Mr. _____:

It was an honor to receive your call offering me the position at (company name). While I know working with you would be a wonderful experience for me, I have chosen to pursue another opportunity at this time. Thank you very much for considering me. I wish you the best of luck in finding the right candidate for the position.

Sincerely,

_____

God gave us our relatives; thank God we can choose our friends.

—ETHEL WATTS MUMFORD, AMERICAN NOVELIST AND PLAYWRIGHT

Chapter 5
SISTERHOODS AND SUPPORT CIRCLES

Thank You for Being a Friend

Sometimes the most precious gifts don't come in a box tied up with a beautiful bow, but are intangible gestures of love and support wrapped in the fabric of the heart. Whether you're going through a bad breakup, recovering from a loss, or embarking on a new adventure or an exciting phase of life, the gifts of kindness, friendship, and understanding are what make our lives richer and sweeter. So the next time you've gotten through with a little help from your friends, let them know how grateful you are for their understanding.

GRATEFUL SAGE TIPS
When someone has done something nice for you, a great way to say thank you is to pay the kindness forward and pass the magic of gratitude on to someone else.

Try including a quote on friendship with your thank-you note. Those poets really do have a way with words!

Ten Things Every Grateful Friend Should Know

1. Do tell your friends how much you appreciate them.
2. Don't take your friends for granted.
3. Do acknowledge the little tokens of support you are given, and give them in return.
4. Don't ever be afraid to tell your friends how you feel. If they walk away, they were never true friends to begin with.
5. Do listen when people speak to you and look them in the eye. Even if you have nothing to say, they will feel you have heard them.
6. Don't ever be jealous of your friends' success, love life, or material possessions. We all have a different path to walk in life, so be inspired to achieve your own triumphs.
7. Do keep your friends' confidences. If your friends have entrusted you with private information, don't be a gossip. It's always wise to keep your personal details to yourself.
8. Don't be afraid to walk away from caustic people who belittle you or make you feel less than who you are.
9. Do encourage your friends to get help if they need it.
10. Do make time to celebrate life, love, and friendship. Eat and be merry with your friends—discover new worlds at museums and boutiques, and go to fabulous destinations!

Writing Thank-Yous of Friendship

It's true that handwritten notes are always best, but when it comes to friendship, saying thank you can take many forms beyond the formalities of pen and paper and social protocol. Often, it is the unexpected thank-you that warms our heart and touches our soul.

* Handwritten cards and notes sent through the mail often surprise the recipient with a burst of appreciation because they really are thoughtful and intimate.

* Small gifts make excellent thank-yous and need not be expensive. If your friend loves to garden, a small package of flower seeds or an herb plant really shows that you were making it personal. The possibilities are endless!

✸ Edible thank-yous are delicious, too, whether homebaked or from the corner bakery or candy shop.

✸ E-mailed thank-yous are always kind, especially ones created with one of the dozens of greeting card Web sites.

✸ Who doesn't adore gorgeous flowers, fabulous chocolate, or festive Champagne? These are always sweet thank-you options!

QUIPS FROM GRATEFUL SAGES THROUGH THE AGES

Friendship with oneself is all-important because without it one cannot be friends with anyone else in the world.

—ELEANOR ROOSEVELT, AMERICAN AUTHOR AND FIRST LADY

It is not so much our friends' help that helps us as the confident knowledge that they will help us.

—EPICURUS, CLASSICAL GREEK PHILOSOPHER

I count myself in nothing else so happy
As in a soul remembering my good friends.

—WILLIAM SHAKESPEARE, ELIZABETHAN POET AND PLAYWRIGHT

Have no friends not equal to yourself.

—CONFUCIUS, CHINESE PHILOSOPHER

The only reward of virtue is virtue; the only way to have a friend is to be one.

—RALPH WALDO EMERSON, TRANSCENDENTALIST WRITER

True friendship is a plant of slow growth, and must undergo and withstand the shocks of adversity before it is entitled to the appellation.

—GEORGE WASHINGTON, FIRST UNITED STATES PRESIDENT

PAY IT FORWARD

GRATITUDE IN ACTION

A great way to say thank you to your friends and family for their help in making your life extra-special is to remember their birthdays and significant events. Calendar software programs and handheld devices that synchronize with your computer make it simple to remember your important dates. Because it's only necessary to enter the birthday, anniversary, or graduation date with the person's contact information once, you are reminded every year without the need to constantly re-enter the information. A flashing alarm pops up so you can't forget.

There are also many websites on the Internet you can register with that will send out e-mails to your friends requesting their current contact, birthday, and anniversary information so you don't have to input and update the information yourself. Then you can set reminder alarms that can be e-mailed to your PDA, computer, or even your phone. Some greeting card websites will even allow you to create e-cards in advance for such things as thank-you notes, just-because notes, care-and-concern cards, or birthday cards. They can then be sent on a specified date, so if you're traveling and can't send your best friend an e-card on her special day, no need to worry, the website will send it for you! Or the event alarm might just propel you to send a real card through the mail!

Thank You for Being a Friend—Sample Notes

Here you will find notes to help you reach out and touch someone who has reached out to you. Use these words of appreciation for the people who have helped you through the rough spots.

THE GLOBAL THANK-YOU THESAURUS

Afrikaans	Dankie
Armenian	Shenorhakal yem
Chinese (Mandarin)	Toa chie
Dutch	Dank je
English	Thank you
French	Merci beaucoup
German	Danke schoen
Greek	Efharistó
Hebrew	To-da
Hungarian	Kösz, Köszönöm
Irish (Gaelic)	Go raibh maith agat
Italian	Grazie
Japanese	Arigato
Norwegian	Takk
Polish	Dziekuje
Portuguese	Obrigado
Spanish	Muchas gracias
Swahili	Asante
Swedish	Tack
Welsh	Diolch

Thanks for Being There

Dear Katie,

How can I ever thank you for always being there for me? You are a true friend, and I am forever grateful. Thank you.

With appreciation,

Emma

Thanks for Being My Greek Sister

Dear _____,

It has been both an honor and a privilege to be your (name of sorority) sister. Through all the exchanges, excitement, studying, and fraternity activity you are someone I always know will be there. Thank you for being in my life.

(sorority name) love,

_____

Thanks for Being My Soul Sister

Dear _____,

We've laughed until we've cried and we've held each other tightly. I feel so blessed that we've walked this life together and shared in each other's joys and sorrows. From the bottom of my heart, thank you for being my sister and my best friend.

Love,

_____

Thanks, Just Because

Dear _____,

I want you to know that you mean the world to me.

Thank you for being my best friend.

With my love,

_____

Dear _____,

There are simply no words to express the depth of my gratitude . . .

Thank you,

_____

Thanks for Our Rock-Solid Friendship

Dear _____,

You are the best! No matter what's happening, you are always someone I can count on through thick and thin. I don't think you'll ever know how much I appreciate your gracious heart and the courageous spirit that always makes me smile. You have affected my life on so many levels. I am truly a better person because of you. Thank you.

Yours truly,

_____

Thanks for Saving Me from Myself

Dear _____,

Thank you for holding me up when I didn't think I was going to make it. Thank you for showing me there really is a light at the end of the tunnel. Thank you for reminding me to count my blessings. Thank you for saving me from my fears and doubts. Thank you for explaining that time heals all wounds. Thank you for just letting me cry. Thank you, my friend.

Love,

_____

Ignorant men don't know what good they hold in their hands until they've flung it away.

—SOPHOCLES, CLASSICAL GREEK PLAYWRIGHT

Chapter 6
LOVE AND ROMANCE

Thank You from the Bottom of My Heart

One of our greatest human needs is to be loved by another and feel appreciated. Romantic scribes have known for centuries that the key to capturing a loved one's heart begins with a passionate letter declaring their love and admiration. With stars in their eyes, they bare their souls, risking rejection to give the gift of gratitude to another hopeful heart. After all, the essence of a love letter is really a proclamation thanking someone for how that person makes you feel. In today's world sometimes lovers forget how key it is to acknowledge the importance of the other person in their lives. Those two small words—"thank you"—are so powerful, they have the ability to make, break, or build a relationship. It is essential that we make a habit of using them daily. So the next time you've got a prince on the line, send him a Thank-You from the Bottom of My Heart note. It's guaranteed to help seal the deal!

GRATEFUL SAGE TIP
If someone sends you flowers, call immediately to say thank you, then send a handwritten note of thanks.

Writing the Romantic Thank-You
When it comes to writing tender notes of love and appreciation there aren't any set rules. The most important thing to do is

simply write down your feelings of gratitude and send them. What matters are the passionate words that come from your heart. Sometimes it feels difficult to express out loud what we feel, or we feel ridiculous writing something that seems overly dramatic or too emotional. But just a few words can have a tremendous impact. You don't have to write pages, even a loving phrase will do.

Ideas to Help Keep Love's Light in Your Life!

❊ Send a handwritten thank-you love note on your favorite stationery. With a quick spray of your perfume, he'll surely think of you. Maybe a sweet lipstick kiss on the envelope will make his heart feel yours, too.

❊ There are hundreds of stationery choices, from creative and funny store-bought cards to elegant finely crafted and handmade paper.

❊ Send a postcard with a short little note, love quote, or poem. He'll get the message!

❊ E-mails and e-cards are always appreciated and add sparkle to your loved one's day. Check out some of the online greeting card websites.

❊ Text messaging is wonderful instant communication to let that special someone know you're thinking of them, too. C U L8R!

❊ Slip a note into your sweetheart's briefcase, pocket, suitcase, or car. He'll be surprised when he finds it and grateful to know you took the time to do something special.

❊ Don't forget that your appreciation can extend beyond a written thank-you note. Hugs, kisses, holding hands, and eye contact are all ways to connect with that gratitude attitude. Actions really can speak louder than words.

GRATEFUL SAGE TIP
Don't think that once you're married the romance is over. It's up to you to keep it alive.

∽

Timing Is Everything

Yes, it is a good thing to demonstrate your feelings, otherwise you'd never know if he feels the same way about you, too. At the same time, you want to be a lady and let the gentleman court you. In the beginning of a relationship, some men might feel a woman is coming on too strongly if she sends a barrage of fan mail, so use your best judgment. You'll know when the time is right.

If you have no intention of seeing a guy again following your first date, then let the verbal "thank you" given at the end of the evening suffice. Don't send an e-mail the next day thanking him again, because he might think you're interested in him. If he follows up and you aren't interested, simply let him know you appreciated the date and don't set up a future one.

On the other hand, if you think you've met your match, wait and see what happens. After a few dates you'll probably have each other's e-mails, and it would be appropriate to send a note saying something thoughtful like,

Sam,

When I said I always wished to have Champagne over New York City, I never dreamed it would come true. Sipping bubbles high atop the Empire State Building was a night I'll never forget. Thank you for caring enough to make my dream come true.

With affection,

Maggie

Acknowledging the effort your potential love interest makes causes that magical gift of gratitude to continue. People want to keep giving when they feel appreciated for their efforts because it makes them feel warm and fuzzy inside. So whatever you decide to do, be creative and do it well so those love blessings keep coming to you!

Ten Relationship Keys Every Girl Should Know

1. Do remember that if you don't love and respect *yourself first* no one else will.
2. Don't try to change someone into what you think the person should be, and don't let anyone try to change you.
3. Do be appreciative and acknowledge even the small efforts your love interest makes.
4. Don't stay in a relationship if you are unhappy or not being treated the way you deserve. Life is simply too short.
5. Do help and support each other without being demanding.
6. Don't be afraid to forgive. It releases your anger and allows you to love again.
7. Do remember it takes work and communication to make a successful relationship last forever.
8. Don't try to rescue someone who needs professional help for bad habits.
9. Do observe how your mate treats others; he will treat you the same way.
10. Do give love generously without expectations.

GRATEFUL SAGE TIP

According to marriage and family therapists Drs. Lew and Gloria Richfield, authors of *Together Forever: 125 Loving Ways to Have a Vital and Romantic Marriage*, "Mail a love letter to your partner. With a stamp. Love letters shouldn't stop just because you live at the same address."

☙

QUIPS FROM GRATEFUL AND AFFECTIONATE SAGES THROUGH THE AGES

The deepest principle in human nature is the craving to be appreciated.

—WILLIAM JAMES, AMERICAN PSYCHOLOGIST AND PHILOSOPHER

Thou art to me a delicious torment.

—RALPH WALDO EMERSON, TRANSCENDENTALIST WRITER

Associate yourself with men of good quality if you esteem your own reputation; for 'tis better to be alone than in bad company.

—GEORGE WASHINGTON, FIRST UNITED STATES PRESIDENT

Men are like wine: some turn to vinegar, but the best improve with age.

—POPE JOHN XXIII

There is no remedy for love but to love more.

—HENRY DAVID THOREAU, AMERICAN AUTHOR

I met in the street a very poor young man who was in love. His hat was old, his coat worn, his cloak was out at the elbows, the water passed through his shoes—and the stars through his soul.

—VICTOR HUGO, FRENCH WRITER AND POET

THE INTERNATIONAL LANGUAGE OF LOVE THESAURUS

English	I love you
French	Je t'aime
German	Ich liebe dich
Greek	S'agapo
Irish (Gaelic)	Ta gra agam ort
Italian	Ti amo
Japanese	Ai'shiteru yo
Polish	Kocham cie
Russian	Ya tebya liubliu
Spanish	Te amo
Swedish	Jag älskar dig
Welsh	Rwy'n dy garu di

GRATEFUL SAGE TIP

My mother always said, "The way to a man's heart is through his stomach." It really is true. Cook a fabulous candlelight dinner, send a basket of homemade chocolate chip cookies, or make a seaside picnic and show him you appreciate him.

SHAKESPEAREAN PHRASES OF
LOVE AND DEVOTION

In thy face I see the map of honor, truth, and loyalty.

—HENRY VI, PART TWO

When I saw you I fell in love, and you smiled because you knew.

—ROMEO AND JULIET

My heart is ever at your service, my lord.

—TIMON OF ATHENS

Love looks not with the eyes, but with the mind;
And therefore is wing'd Cupid painted blind.

—A MIDSUMMER NIGHT'S DREAM

Now join your hands, and with your hands your hearts.

—KING HENRY VI

They do not love that do not show their love.

—TWO GENTLEMEN OF VERONA

The course of true love never did run smooth.

—A MIDSUMMER NIGHT'S DREAM

Thank You from the Bottom of My Heart—Sample Notes
When it comes to love and romance, there's nothing like a
well-timed thank-you note to rekindle an old flame, ignite a
new one, or let Mr. Right's parents know you're the one.

Thank You for Loving Me

Dear _____,

*You make me feel like I'm the only woman in this whole wide
world. Thank you for loving me.*

Love,

_____

Dear _____,

*There are simply no words to express how grateful I am to
have you in my life . . .*
With all my love and affection,

_____

Thank You for Being My Friend

Dear _____,

*Thank you for loving me for who I am and never, ever trying
to change me. Thank you for allowing me the freedom to
pursue my dreams and showing me I really can do anything.
Thank you for applauding my victories and catching me
when I fall. Thank you for being my friend. I adore you.*
Love,

_____

Thank You for the Flowers

Dear Tommy,

What a wonderful surprise! When those beautiful flowers
came down the hall I really thought they were for someone else.
They were so stunning I couldn't believe it when they stopped at
my desk—then I saw my name on the card. My heart pounded
and swelled with emotion when I read your sweet words.
Thank you for making me the most envied woman in the office!
I love you, too . . .
Elizabeth

Thank You, Just Because

Dear Aric,

When I was a little girl I dreamed about what you'd be like.
I looked into the heavens every night and wondered where you
were and how and when we'd meet. I begged the stars to keep
you safe and for the moon to light your way to me. As I stand
next to you now and gaze into your eyes, I am so incredibly
thankful I met you that starry, starry night.
With all my love,
Kelly

Thank You to Mr. Right's Parents

This kind of thank-you note would lend itself to an air of higher formality than a casual love note.

Dear Mr. and Mrs. Jin,

It has been such a pleasure getting to know both of you over this past year. I really appreciate your welcoming me into your home and always including me in your family plans. I especially enjoyed helping in the kitchen and cooking that delicious (name of holiday) dinner. Thank you for making me feel so special.

Sincerely yours,

Jessica Pierce

Thank You for the Gift

Dear _____,

I am forever grateful to you for your thoughtful and generous gift. I know it comes from your gracious heart to mine. A thousand kisses . . .

Love,

_____

Thank You for Dinner

Dear_____,

*How do you always think of the most wonderful things to do?
I loved having dinner with you last night at (name of
place/beach/park). It was such a fun idea and I really, really
enjoyed being with you. Thank you for making it an amazing
evening.*

With affection,

_____

Thank You for Loving Me, Good-Bye

Dear _____,

*This note is hard for me to write because I love you. I have
felt so honored to have you in my life, and I'm grateful to
have gotten the chance to know you. I wish our timing was
different, because if we had met in another place and time,
who knows what could have been? Thank you for loving me
so much, you're willing to let me go. I will remember you
always.*

Love,

_____

Let us be grateful to people who make us happy. They are the charming gardeners who make our souls blossom.

—MARCEL PROUST, FRENCH NOVELIST

Chapter 7

WEDDING BELLS AND THANK-YOUS

I Do, I Do, and Thank You, Too

From the moment we brides say "yes," we're swept up in a white wave of wedding traditions and rituals, parties, and presents, all of which require thank-you notes. At this time, probably more than at any other, we have a great deal to be thankful for. That means writing a huge number of thank-you notes! Don't be selfish and write them all yourself; let your groom share in writing them, too. From the engagement party to the bachelorette party, the bridal shower, the wedding, the honeymoon, and beyond into the first year of marriage, we are expressing our gratitude and appreciation for the support, love, and generosity that we enjoy from our friends and family at this special time.

The Grateful Bride's Guide to Thank-You Success

The last thing you want to think about at your reception or on your honeymoon is the mountain of thank-you notes that have to be sent out upon your return home. It can be utterly overwhelming. By taking just a few simple steps before the big day, you can really reduce the worry and feel free to dance the night away without a single twinge of bridal-gratitude guilt. At your shower you probably had someone writing down everything you received and the name of the sender. After the wedding, it is often difficult to be so organized. There is no way in the world you will be able to remember who gave you what gift and when. Here are a few ideas to help you avoid bridal-gratitude guilt.

❋ Many brides keep a bride's file that contains 3″ × 5″ index cards for each invited guest with all their pertinent contact information. Other brides keep a list of gifts received and thank-you notes sent. If you can't find the time to do either of these, simply take the gift card and mark the date you received the gift, what the gift is, and the address of the sender. You can also cut the return address from the box or envelope and tape or staple it to the gift card. This trick really helped me!

❋ After you write the thank-you note, mark the card with a check or star and include the date, in case you need to go back and check that you sent the note.

❋ Keep all your cards that need acknowledgment and thank-you notes in one place. Try to do a few every day so you don't get overwhelmed. (Don't forget, people can send you gifts for up to a year.) Better yet, get your new spouse to write a few with you. Open a bottle of bubbly, order in, and make it fun!

❋ Use one of your gift boxes for the gift cards that need thank-you notes and another one for the ones you've sent.

❋ Order or purchase your stationery in advance so you're ready to go when you return from your honeymoon. Get a package of nice ink pens at the same time so you're not scrambling for something to write with.

The Grateful Bride's Thank-You Checklist
1. Traditionally the bridal thank-you note is formal and always handwritten.
2. The wedding thank-you note should be sent within three months of the event.
3. The appropriate stationery to use is of good quality and is ecru or white in color with a matching envelope. Pastel colors have also become acceptable.
4. The traditional bride's fold-over or "informal" note is approximately 5¼″ wide × 3½″ high and is typically personalized with your name or monogram.

5. Write out a draft of what you want to say before writing the actual note. Because brides have so many notes to write, you can use the same note and revise it by personalizing it for each individual.

6. You'll be writing a lot of notes, so there is a tendency to become repetitive, which can make your note sound stale and generic. Use "The Thank-You Thesaurus" to give yourself some fresh ideas. There are many ways to say the same thing, only better!

7. Always double-check the spelling of the person's name and address.

8. Use lined paper underneath your note so your writing forms a straight line. You can also use a ruler or anything with a straight edge to guide your pen. And leave yourself room on the page—don't jam it all together!

9. Before you seal the envelope, read your note out loud to make sure you didn't miss a word or two.

10. If you have a large wedding with hundreds of guests, consider sending out "gift acknowledgment" cards, so the person sending the gift knows it has been received and that a thank-you note is on the way. This gives you more time to write a proper thank-you note.

11. Always use black or blue ink to write your thank-yous! It looks elegant and shows you have class and style. Avoid using metallic or rainbow colors.

12. Don't send e-mail thank-you notes for wedding gifts. They are inappropriate and unacceptable.

13. Don't use your bad handwriting as an excuse not to send a thank-you! If you absolutely must, you can use a computer software script font like Monotype Corsiva and print your thank-you notes, then personally sign them.

14. Brides should sign with their maiden name before the wedding and married name (if they are using it) after the wedding.

Avoiding Late Thank-You Note Anxiety

If it happens that somehow you missed sending a thank-you note within that three-month period or close to it, try to be gracious about the error. Write something like:

❋ "In all the excitement of the wedding I somehow managed to separate your gift from your card…" or "Many apologies for the tardiness of my note. As you can imagine, we are still getting used to married life…"

❋ Don't delay your thank-you note with the excuse that you're waiting to include your wedding picture. Just send it!

❋ Call the person who ships you a gift so the person isn't left wondering if it arrived. It really deflates gift givers if you don't acknowledge the spirit of excitement they are expecting you to have when you receive their present.

Monogram

Monograms are always in style and represent a certain sense of tradition and class. Don't be afraid to use them; they add elegance to the presentation of your thank-you note.

Before the wedding, you would use your first, middle, and maiden name.

Caitlin Rose Poisson

If you're using initials that are all the same height, they should follow the order of your name. Your monogram would look like this: *CRP*.

If you're using initials that vary in height, your last name would be in the middle: *CPR*.

After the wedding, your new last name is incorporated into
your monogram. Your maiden name will move into the
position of your middle name, and your married name will take
the place of your maiden name.

Caitlin Poisson Shoup

If you are using initials of the same size, your new
monogram would look like this: *CPS*.
With initials of different heights, your new initial (for your
married name) will be in the middle: *CSP*.

The Electronic Thank-You

If you're thinking about sending out cyber thank-you notes for
your wedding gifts, stop right where you are! Only the classic,
handwritten thank-you note is acceptable for this momentous
occasion. Blanket thank-yous are definitely not appropriate,
nor does an enthusiastic posting on your wedding website
substitute for thanking each and every person individually for
their generous gift to you.

Returning Gifts

Even though you registered, it's inevitable that someone will
give you something that simply isn't your style and must be
returned. Here are some ideas to handle this delicately:

1. Avoid telling the gift giver unless the item is broken or
   damaged. Do your best to return the gift to the store of
   purchase; hold on to the packaging if there is no gift receipt.
2. Really consider the gift giver's feelings before you return a gift.
   If the gift is from your new mother-in-law, you might want to
   consider holding on to it to foster good family relations.
3. If you can't return or exchange the gift, consider donating
   it to someone who would cherish it.
4. As a last resort, try reselling the item; www.ebay.com is a
   wonderful selling tool.

I Do, I Do, and Thank You, Too—Sample Notes
Here are some thank-you notes to help you let everybody in
your extended wedding party know how much their
contribution to your new life means to both of you.

Thank You to the Bride's Parents for the Wedding

Dear Mom and Dad,

*We are simply overwhelmed by the beautiful wedding you
gave Philip and me. I dreamt of this day my entire life but
never envisioned the spectacular event that would take place.
It was truly a wedding that far exceeded our expectations.
We thank you from the bottom of our hearts for giving us our
dream. Thank you for every single detail and for
understanding when I might have been . . . impatient! But
more important, thank you for all of your love and support.*

With all my love,

Margaret

China

Dear _____,

*We are overwhelmed by your generous gift. You couldn't
possibly imagine how many china patterns we looked at
before we finally picked this one. We will think of you both
every time we use our fabulous china on every celebration,
special occasion, and holiday. Thank you.*

Sincerely,

_____

Cookware

Dear Dr. and Mrs. Katz,

We just can't thank you enough for the spectacular cookware!
You know we love to cook, and with all the cookbooks we
received, we're sure to be in fierce competition with world-class
chefs. Now we can make all the very best gourmet meals. After
we've had a chance to practice a recipe or two, we'd love to
have you both over for dinner. Robert joins me in thanking you.
Sincerely yours,
Yvette

Crystal Glassware

Dear Mr. and Mrs. Genders,

When I met (name of groom), I felt as though I had stumbled
upon the most sparkling thing in the world. That is, until I
opened your gift last night. Thank you for the crystal
glasses—they are just magnificent. We were so excited to use
them, we opened a very special bottle of Champagne on the
spot and toasted you for your love and thoughtfulness! Cheers!
Love,
Toni Vrdoljak

Fill-in-the-Blanks

Dear Mr. and Mrs. _____,

The one thing we desperately needed was _____. You would not believe how many times we have already used it this week alone. Thank you so much, we just love it! More important, thank you for sharing our special day with us.

Sincerely,

_____

Dear Mr. and Mrs. Manning,

I know I thanked you at the reception, but I just wanted to let you both know again how much we appreciate the lovely (fill in) you gave us. We hope you had a wonderful time at our wedding . . . it meant so much to us to have you there. Thank you.

With affection,

Patsy

Candlesticks

Dear Martin,

Harvey joins me in thanking you for the gorgeous candlesticks! We just love them. We will think of you over every romantic candlelight dinner . . . well, not every one! Thank you so very much.

With love,

Christina

Frame

Dear Mr. and Mrs. Jayes,

Thank you so much for the beautiful frame! We really wanted a special one for our wedding picture, and this one is just stunning. Please know that when we look at it, we will think of your generosity. We hope you had a wonderful time at the wedding and thank you for joining us.

Most sincerely,

Ella

Gift Certificates and Gift Cards

Dear _____,

You can't imagine our excitement when we opened your gift! Thank you so much for your very generous gift certificate. With all the things we want to set up our new home, now we can go on a shopping spree and get everything we need. We are just thrilled! From the bottom of our hearts, thank you.

Gratefully yours,

_____

GRATEFUL SAGE TIP

Crane's *Blue Book of Stationery* (Doubleday), is an excellent resource for all brides!

Platter

Dear Kelsea and Jack,

What a gorgeous platter! No matter what we serve on it, it's going to look delicious, and that's half the battle! We love it and look forward to using it at our next festive occasion . . . after we recover. Thank you so much for thinking of us and for being such good friends.

Sincerely,

Mick

Silver

Dear Betty and Dee,

Chris and I screamed when we opened your "sterling" gift. We absolutely love the silver_____! We just can't express how grateful we are; (it is/they are) simply lovely. We will definitely enjoy (it/them) on each and every special occasion. Thank you!

Sincerely yours,

Carolyn

Vase

Dear Mr. and Mrs. Bercsi,

You can't imagine how excited we were when we opened your gift. The one thing we really wanted was crystal! The vase is so stunning that it immediately went up on the mantel over the fireplace. Now we have a really great excuse to keep the living room filled with beautiful flowers. Thank you so much for thinking of us and helping us celebrate our wedding.

With love,

Katie Sterling

Reverend, Priest, Rabbi

Dear Father Joe,

It is with great joy that I write this note to thank you for performing the wedding ceremony for Michael and me. We so appreciated the time you took meeting with us and making sure that every element of the ceremony was just right. I know that marriage can be trying at times, but we truly feel that with the tools of honor, communication, and trust you have shared with us, we are sure to be prepared for anything that comes our way. Thank you so very much for cementing our bond to each other.

Respectfully yours,

Wendy Fish

Groom's Parents—Rehearsal Dinner

Dear Mom and Dad,

The rehearsal dinner you gave for _____ and me was magnificent in every way. A special night, surrounded by only our closest of family and friends, that filled our hearts with joy. As you both rose to toast us, my heart raced with excitement at the prospect of my new life. Thank you for everything you've done to give me my wonderful life. But more important, thank you for showing me how to love, through the way you love each other.

Love,

_____

Maid and Matron of Honor, Bridesmaids

Dear Stephanie,

I can't believe this moment has finally come. Do you remember looking up into the stars and thinking, "somewhere the man I will marry is looking at these stars, too, but where is he?!!" In the blink of an eye, it seems, that moment arrived. We sure kissed a lot of frogs to find a real prince. I want to thank you for always being there for me every single time my heart broke or I cried with joy. I treasure our friendship and thank you for standing beside me on my very special wedding day.

Love,

Aurélie

Happily Ever After Anniversary Gifts

YEAR	TRADITIONAL	MODERN
1	Paper	Clock
2	Cotton	China
3	Leather	Crystal, Glass
4	Linen (Silk)	Appliances
5	Wood	Silverware
6	Candy or Iron	Wooden objects
7	Wool (Copper)	Desk sets
8	Bronze	Linens, Lace
9	Pottery (Willow)	Leather goods
10	Tin, Aluminum	Diamond
11	Steel	Fashion jewelry
12	Silk (Linen)	Pearls, Colored gems
13	Lace	Textiles, Furs
14	Ivory	Gold jewelry
15	Crystal	Watches
16	Silver	Hollowware
17		Furniture
18		Porcelain
19		Bronze
20	China	Platinum
21		Brass, Nickel
22		Copper
23		Silverplate
24		Musical instruments
25	Silver	Sterling silver
26		Original artwork
27		Sculpture
28		Orchids
29		New furniture
30	Pearl	Diamond
31		Timepieces
32		Conveyances (automobiles)
33		Amethyst
34		Opal
35	Coral (Jade)	Jade
40	Ruby	Ruby
45	Sapphire	Sapphire
50	Gold	Gold

To speak gratitude is courteous and pleasant, to enact gratitude is generous and noble, but to live gratitude is to touch Heaven.

—JOHANNES A. GAERTNER, GERMAN AUTHOR AND POET

Chapter 8
THANK YOU, BABY!

Baby Showers, Christenings, and First Birthdays

When you are getting ready to welcome a new addition to the family, the demands of pregnancy and preparing for a baby can make it difficult just to keep up with your busy schedule. In addition to all the anticipation, there are also hundreds of thank-you notes to write before, during, and after the baby, and for months to come. Just when you think you've received your last gift and sent off your final thank-you note, you get another present! Still, it's important to let your friends and family know how much you appreciate their love, support, and generosity during this special time. So if you're expecting or adopting, here are some suggestions and sample thank-yous to help you express your gratitude without exhausting yourself.

GRATEFUL SAGE TIPS

It's a good idea to pass along the gift of "thank you" to your children and teach them how to write their own thank-you notes once they're able to write.

You can order special postage stamps with your baby's picture on them!

QUIPS FROM GRATEFUL SAGES THROUGH THE AGES
༄

May there be a generation of children
On the children of your children.

—IRISH BLESSING

God could not be everywhere and therefore he made mothers.

—JEWISH PROVERB

Feeling gratitude and not expressing it is like wrapping a present
and not giving it.

—WILLIAM ARTHUR WARD, AMERICAN WRITER AND POET

Just to be is a blessing. Just to live is holy.

—RABBI ABRAHAM JOSHUA HESCHEL, JEWISH THEOLOGIAN

Ten Things Every Grateful New Mom Should Know

1. If you're ordering birth announcements, buy your thank-you notes at the same time. It's one less thing you'll have to worry about.

2. Just about everything—from personalized thank-you notes, postage stamps, ink pens, and even what you'll need for the baby—can be ordered online.

3. It's a good rule to send out your thank-you notes within two weeks, but if you miss the time frame, add something like, "With the sleepless nights of our precious new baby, all the days have rolled into one…"

4. After the baby is born, it's likely more presents and flowers will come. Even though everyone understands that you just had a baby, they still expect a thank-you note.

5. It's always a good idea to call the person who sent you flowers so they are matched with the same level of

enthusiasm in which they were sent. If you aren't up to it, then have your husband or friend call on your behalf.

6. If you get flowers in the hospital, make sure you bring the gift cards home with you so you won't forget to send a note later.

7. You will get things you won't need. If you can't return or exchange them, consider donating the items to someone who does need them.

8. Keep the gift cards, and note the item on the back. Mark it with a check or star when you've sent your thank-you note, and put the gift cards in your baby box.

9. Make sure especially to thank all the people in your life who went through your pregnancy and put up with you during your mood swings and midnight cravings, too. And if you're adopting, thank all the people who helped bring that little miracle into your arms.

10. Always remember the importance of your health and your baby's. Don't let your thank-you notes stress you out. If you are feeling overwhelmed, write one a day until they are finished. Keep in mind that having a baby isn't an everyday occurrence, so cherish this time.

GRATEFUL SAGE TIP

Wait before removing the tags on baby clothes and keep gift receipts until after the baby is born. You may have a boy instead of a girl, or your baby may be much bigger than expected, and you may need to make some exchanges.

⤜✄⤏

NINE DO'S AND DON'TS FOR EXPECTANT MOMS

1. Do get your thank-you note stationery before your baby shower.

2. Do pick up postage stamps ahead of time or order them online.

3. Do ask someone at your shower to make a list of every gift you receive and write down who gave it.

4. Do consider picking up a nice name and address book so your guests can write down their current contact information.

5. Don't forget to send a thank-you note to the person who hosted the shower for you.

6. Do handwrite your notes and keep them looking as elegant and gracious as possible.

7. Do remember to refer to "Thank-You Notes 101" for your thank-you note guidelines.

8. Do start writing and sending out your notes as soon as possible.

9. Don't ever use e-mail to send out your baby thank-you notes.

Baby Showers—Sample Thank-You Notes

Baby Monitor

Dear Robin and David,

It was so thoughtful of you to send us a gift for Ryan and Jackson. I had no idea I would be so nervous each and every single time I stepped out of the babies' room for fear I wouldn't hear them crying. Having your gift of a baby monitor has given me the freedom to do the normal daily things, like taking a shower! Now my mind is at ease, knowing I will be able to listen to my little ones and be there when they need me, no matter where I am in the house! Thank you!

Sincerely yours,

Marilyn

Car Seat

Dear Mrs. Reynoso,

What a thoughtful gift you gave me. Just think, the very first thing the baby will be nestled in as he leaves the hospital for a safe journey home is your car seat. Thank you for the one thing I needed most! Even more important, thank you for being with me at my shower. Your presence made the day that much more special to me. Thank you.

With affection,

Louise Cueva

Blanket

Dear Linda, Frank, Laura, and Michelle,
I absolutely adore the beautiful satin receiving blanket and
am looking forward to using it. I still can't believe that very
soon I will have a cute little bundle of joy! Thank you so much
for such a lovely and thoughtful gift to snuggle the baby in. I
know the baby will love it as much as I do.
With love,
Rachel

Money, Stock, Savings Bonds

Dear Robert, Riley, and Dylan,
Thank you so much for your generous check for the baby. We
have decided to (put it in/open up) the baby's savings
account. Please know it will be put to good use and help ensure
him a good education. Thank you for your thoughtfulness and
for giving our little one just what he needed.
With much love,
Colleen

Clothing

Dear Aunt Norma,
I just wanted to thank you again for the beautiful things you
gave us for Emily. They are all lovely and certainly arrived
in the nick of time. She is already wearing the _____,

dripping milk all over herself, and quite honestly being the most beautiful baby I could have ever wished for. Thank you so much for thinking of us, Aunt Norma, we really appreciate it. Please send our love to Uncle Warren.

Love,

Brenda

Stroller

Dear Aunt Patty,

Oh, you shouldn't have, but we are so thankful you did! We love the (brand name) stroller for the baby. It will take us from the baby stages all the way past those toddler years and then some! Now I will be able to stroll down the avenue and shop while my little one relaxes in total luxury. Thank you so much! I love it! With affection,

Megan

Baby Book or Photo Album

Dear _____,

Your presence at my shower was a gift in itself. Thank you for the gorgeous (baby book/photo album). I am really looking forward to filling the pages and capturing every single moment the baby does anything. Thank you again for all your love and support. With my love,

_____

Fill-in-the-Blanks

Dear Jill, Tom, and Alex,

What an incredible surprise it was to open the front door this afternoon and find a big box addressed to me. I love the _____! That was definitely one thing I absolutely needed to have for our little one. Thank you for such a lovely and thoughtful gift.

With love,

Nicole

Grandparents

Dear Mom,

I just want to thank you for all the help and advice you have given me with the baby. Just knowing you are there to lend a shoulder to cry on and call for help in the middle of the night when the baby is crying . . . well, screaming . . . has been a godsend for me. I only hope I am as wonderful a mother as you have been to me. I love you and thank you always.

Love,

Kelly

P.S. When can you baby-sit?

Shower Hostess

Dear Gina and Elena,

Words cannot express how much I appreciate you both giving me a baby shower. It was truly the best party I have ever been to. From the tiny party favors to the delicious pink and blue cupcakes, everything was simply perfect. Thank you for making me feel so wonderful. I am blessed to have you in my life.

Love,

Janice

Christening—Sample Thank-You Notes

When you're celebrating baby's christening, here are some heavenly notes to help you show your appreciation for baby's blessings.

Fill-in-the-Blanks

Dear David and Sara,

What an honor it was to have you celebrate Savannah and David's christening with us. We were simply thrilled when we opened your gift. Please know the _____ is something that we are certain the children will cherish for a lifetime. Thank you for your kindness and blessings.

Love,

Veronica

Dear Aunt Terese, Uncle Rick, and Lily,

Thank you so very much for joining my family to celebrate
my special christening day. I simply adore the _____
you gave me and I will think of all of you every time I see it.
More important, I so appreciate all of the love and support
you have given to my family. From my little heart, I thank
you. May God bless you and your family.

With love,

Anna

Officiating Priest, Reverend, or Father

Dear Monsignor Padric Loftus,

You are indeed a very special and holy man to us. We want you
to know that you have affected not only our lives but also the
lives of the families in our parish community. We are so
grateful to you and the service you have given in God's name.
We humbly thank you for initiating our child into God's divine
grace through baptism and welcoming him into the Church.

Yours faithfully,

Kelly Browne

First Birthdays—Sample Thank-You Notes

Baby's first birthday is always an exciting event as we look
back on the first year of this incredible little life and know we
will cherish those moments forever. Here you'll find a few
thank-you notes you can copy, modify, or use as your own to
help you focus on the real blessing in your life—your baby!

Airplane, Train, Rocket, Toy

Dear Joanna and Christopher,

*Thank you both for celebrating my first birthday with me. I
really appreciate the (airplane/train/rocket/toy) you gave me,
too. It was the one thing I wanted and I look forward to
playing with it every day! I appreciate your generosity.*

Your friend,

Taylor Hamermesh

Arts and Crafts

Dear Uncle Gary, Aunt Rosanna, Ethan, and Seth,

It was so wonderful to see you all at my birthday party. I really enjoyed opening your present and discovering the (arts and crafts item) you gave me! As a matter of fact, I am already making fabulous things, and my mother is delighted I am working on my creativity—as long as I'm outside.

Thank you for such an imaginative gift!

With affection,

Melody

Fill-in-the-Blanks

Dear _____,

I just wanted to thank you for coming to my birthday party. It was so wonderful to have you there to celebrate with me. I love the _____ you gave me. It is the perfect thing for me to play with! Thank you so much for your thoughtfulness.

Sincerely,

_____

Dear _____,

You can't imagine my excitement when I opened your gift! I love the _____ *and am already enjoying playing with it. Thank you so much for your generosity and for thinking of me on my birthday.*

Love,

_____

Gift Cards

Dear _____,

What a pleasure it was to have you celebrate my birthday with me. I loved the _____ *gift cards you gave me, too! I look forward to going shopping and picking out all my favorite things. Thank you for a very special gift.*

With affection,

_____

It's Thank-You Day! If you haven't told somebody lately, now is the time.

—OPRAH WINFREY, TALK-SHOW HOST

Chapter 9

BELATED THANKS AND GESTURES OF APPRECIATION

It's Never Too Late to Say Thank You

Even gracious girls get so wrapped up in the swirl of life that we put off sending thank-you notes. As the weeks rush by, we find ourselves worrying about our tardiness and wondering how we can ever say thank you, now that so much time has passed. There are also those occasions when we realize how influential the kindness of a teacher really was or how essential the deep loyalty of a friend, and we wish we could turn back the clock so we could thank that person properly for making a difference in our lives. The good news is—it's never too late to say thank you.

Writing the Belated Thank-You Note

The format of your thank-you note should match the formality of the event or spirit in which the gift, favor, or kindness was given. Weddings typically require a formal note of thanks, as do social occasions. Just because your note is late is no reason to skip appropriate etiquette. Handwritten notes are always preferred, and if your thank-you is late to the point of embarrassment, avoid sending an e-mail. If you were going to send an e-mail thank-you note, you wouldn't have been so late in doing it! So take a minute, sit down, and write that thank you!

Ten Good Reasons Why It's Never Too Late to Say Thank You

1. Because it's never too late to thank someone for making a difference in your life.
2. Because it's the right thing to do!
3. Because everyone wants to feel appreciated.
4. Because even late thank-yous are powerful, especially when the gift giver thinks the gift or gesture was forgotten.
5. Because sometimes people have no idea how meaningful their life's contributions have been until you tell them.
6. Because the gift of gratitude has the ability to affect people's lives, no matter how late it is.
7. Because not saying thank you can damage your relationships and reputation.
8. Because the un-thanked person may stop giving to you and others.
9. Because people will remember the kind of person you were long after you're gone.
10. Because a late thank-you is better than none at all.

GRATEFUL SAGE TIP

If it's possible, thank the person on the spot for the gift or the favor, then send a follow-up note of thanks. Getting into the habit of graciously saying thank you immediately will help, in case there's any kind of delay in sending out a note.

❦

QUIPS FROM GRATEFUL SAGES THROUGH THE AGES

∽

In the end, we will remember not the words of our enemies, but the silence of our friends.

—DR. MARTIN LUTHER KING JR., AMERICAN CIVIL RIGHTS LEADER

At times our own light goes out and is rekindled by a spark from another person. Each of us has cause to think with deep gratitude of those who have lighted the flame within us.

—ALBERT SCHWEITZER, NOBEL LAUREATE

Silent gratitude isn't much use to anyone.

—GLADYS BRONWYN STERN, ENGLISH NOVELIST

Let us rise up and be thankful, for if we didn't learn a lot today, at least we learned a little, and if we didn't learn a little, at least we didn't get sick, and if we got sick, at least we didn't die; so, let us all be thankful.

—BUDDHA, ENLIGHTENED TEACHER

O Lord that lends me life, lend me a heart replete with thankfulness!

—WILLIAM SHAKESPEARE, ELIZABETHAN POET AND PLAYWRIGHT

GRATEFUL SAGE TIP

"The Bag of a Million Thank-Yous." A wonderful way to acknowledge an important person or teacher in your life is to initiate a box, bag, or scrapbook filled with thank-you notes from friends, parents, students, and faculty. This kind of gift is a priceless keepsake.

SIX DO'S AND DON'TS FOR TARDY THANK-YOUS

1. Do send your thank-you note as soon as you remember. If you don't, you might put it off again.

2. Don't ever say you were too busy to thank someone for thinking of you.

3. Do try to capture the same excitement in which you received the gift or gesture.

4. Don't belabor the apologies for your tardiness in your note.

5. Do keep your note upbeat.

6. Do follow all the rules in writing your thank-yous!

It's Never Too Late to Say Thank You—Sample Notes

We've heard our parents say a million times over, "Did you send a thank-you note?" That simple reminder conjures up panic and fear to the point that, for many of us, the grateful feeling for the gift is lost and the thank-you note forgotten. So for all you thank-you procrastinators, here are some belated thank-you notes that will help you recapture the moment and let the people in your past know you *are* grateful for their generosity.

Thank You for Being My Mentor

Dear Dr. Schultheiss,

There are simply no words to express how grateful I am to you for being my mentor. Thank you for sharing with me your life and your hard-earned advice. I am so tremendously appreciative. I only hope that one day I can repay the honor.

Sincerely,

Terrance Anderson

Dear Mr. Penhallow,

For years I have admired your work not only as a talented novelist and Shakespearean actor but also as one of the community's most charitable men. Through your tireless dedication you have shown me how essential it is in life to love what you do and never, ever, settle for less than what you deserve. Thank you for guiding my way.

Gratefully yours,

William Moran

Thank You, Old Friend

Dear _____,

So many times I think of you and the time we spent together. I wish we could walk back in time, even if only for a moment, and be (age) again. Thank you for being my friend during the good, bad, and in-between. Please know that no matter where life takes us, I will never forget how wonderful you were to me. I wish you love and happiness.

Gratefully yours,

_____

Thank You, Teacher or Room Parent

Dear Mr. Wileman,

What a wonderful year we have had together! I wanted to take a moment to thank you for all of your hard work and dedication throughout the year. I know firsthand how hard you worked to finish each special project for the children. Their eyes glowed with such excitement every time you created something wonderful for them. Thank you is simply not enough. Please know you have left an indelible mark on their memories that they will treasure for a lifetime. Thank you a million times!

With sincere appreciation,

Mary Jane

Thank You for the Gift

Dear _____,

Although I thanked you in person for the (name of gift) you gave me, I wanted you to know how sincerely grateful I am to you for your thoughtfulness. In fact, every time I see it I think of you and how blessed I am to have you in my life. Thank you for thinking of me.

Sincerely yours,

_____

Dear _____,

I have no excuses! Regardless of my tardiness, I absolutely loved the (name of gift) you sent me. Now that I have it, I don't know how I ever survived without it. Thank you so very much for taking the time to find me the perfect gift.

With my appreciation,

_____

Thank You, Teacher

Dear Miss Punzalan,

This "Bag of A Million Thank-Yous" is filled with thank-you notes from the faculty, children, and their parents, all of whom were quite taken with the love, creativity, and tireless dedication you gave to your class and our school. Thank you for giving our precious children memories that will last a lifetime. We salute and applaud your tireless efforts.

Sincerely yours,

Barbara Krueger

Thank You for Making a Difference in My Life

Dear Kelleen,

There are times in our life when we are utterly unaware of the effect we have on someone else. I don't know what I would have done without you. There are simply no words to express how grateful I am to you for your kindness, loyalty, love, and selflessness. You have a lifelong friend in me.

With my sincere thanks,

Mark

Dear Mr. Aston,

There is no way I could go back in time and thank you for everything. But I have this moment. I humbly thank you, from the bottom of my heart to the heavens above, for making a difference in my life. I am forever grateful.

Yours truly,

Chris

Thank You, Dad

Dear Dad,

You are the kind of father every girl dreams of having. Beyond compare, you are the kind of man by which others are measured. Intelligent, accomplished, creative, and handsome— I am so blessed to call you my father. Thank you for always being there and loving me. I adore you.

Love,

Greta

Thank You, Mom

Dear Mom,

Thank you for making me do the things I didn't want to do because they were good for me. Thank you for having the wisdom and patience to let me make mistakes I could learn from. Thank you for encouraging me to finish school when I wanted to see the world. Thank you for holding me through every broken heart. Thank you for making me the woman I am today. Thank you for being my mother. I love you.

Love,

Ava

GRATEFUL SAGE TIP

Did you know that Crane & Company has been around since 1776, when Stephen Crane's mill sold Paul Revere the paper to issue the first Colonial banknotes? To this day Crane & Company manufactures the paper for much of our worldwide currency.

One single grateful thought raised to heaven is the most perfect prayer.

—GOTTHOLD EPHRAIM LESSING, GERMAN DRAMATIST

Chapter 10

FAREWELL, MY FRIEND

For Your Kindness and Sympathy— Thank You from the Heart

There comes a time in all our lives when we must say good-bye to a loved one or dear friend. Whether the departure is anticipated or unexpected, it is one of the most heart-wrenching moments we may ever have to endure. It is the support, love, and sympathy we receive from our friends and family that helps us make it through the day when we feel as if we can't go on. With the help of friends and loved ones we eventually heal, and over time we are able to laugh again without bursting into tears. Remember, life is a journey, and the people we meet along the way may only be there for a moment, but they linger forever in our hearts, never to be forgotten. It is important that we show appreciation to the people who are so meaningful to our lives while we have the chance to do so. Then, when the time does come to say farewell, we feel satisfied in knowing the person we loved so dearly knew it and was recognized.

Writing the Sympathy Thank-You Note

The moment will come when you are ready to write your thank-you notes for the support you received following the passing of a loved one. All of the basic rules of writing thank-you notes apply, however there are no restrictions on sending them by a certain time. It's best to keep formality and elegance in your notes as you honor the departed. Remember, too, that many of the people you are writing your thank-you notes to are also grieving. Thank-yous should be sent to everyone who helped you get through this period of time, including clergy and anyone who sent a gift or condolence card, served as a pallbearer, provided assistance, sent flowers, or made a financial contribution or donation to charity in your loved one's memory.

Ten Sympathetic Sage Tips

1. Do have someone help you if you are unable to write the thank-you notes yourself.
2. Do include the deceased's memorial card in your thank-you note. It is a special keepsake for the people who can't attend the memorial or funeral. These can be easily ordered through the funeral home.
3. Do send a personal handwritten thank-you for flowers received, donations to charity, financial contributions, meals dropped off, or just a shoulder to cry on.
4. Do check into the preprinted thank-you sympathy cards that are available in stationery stores and online, or have someone pick up a box for you.
5. Do consider using personalized sympathy acknowledgment cards that you can order online or through your local stationery store.
6. Do write a few words of personal thanks in preprinted sympathy cards.
7. Don't send e-mailed sympathy thank-you notes!
8. Do consider sending sympathy acknowledgment cards following the death of a prominent person when writing individual thank-you notes for often hundreds of gifts, cards, and donations might be prohibitive.
9. Do consider a tribute to the deceased in your local newspaper when a public acknowledgment is necessary.
10. Don't hesitate to send a condolence note to a friend who's suffered the loss of a friend or family member. Expressions of sympathy are always appropriate.

PAY IT FORWARD WITH LOVE AND HONOR

GRATITUDE IN ACTION

The next time you say farewell to someone you love, start a new tradition. Ask your friends and loved ones to write a note or letter about what that person meant to them. It could be a few words or even a story. Keep the notes together or make a treasured memorial book. Long after the flowers have faded and people have returned to their lives, it will be these memories you will cherish for a lifetime.

QUIPS FROM SYMPATHETIC SAGES THROUGH THE AGES

May the road rise to meet you.
May the wind be always at your back.
May the sun shine warm upon your face.
And rains fall soft upon your fields.
And until we meet again,
May God hold you in the hollow of His hand.

—IRISH BLESSING

Our life is made by the death of others.

—LEONARDO DA VINCI, ITALIAN RENAISSANCE MAN

It is worth dying to find out what life is.

—T. S. ELIOT, ENGLISH POET, DRAMATIST, AND NOBEL LAUREATE

The boundaries between life and death are at best shadowy and vague. Who shall say where one ends and where the other begins?

—EDGAR ALLAN POE, AMERICAN WRITER AND POET

International Customs for Honoring the Departed

Not all cultures regard death as a sad occasion. Some regard it as an exciting event that is part of our circle of life.

❀ Ancient Egyptians revered death because it began their journey to the afterlife. Considerable time and effort were spent in the preparation of funeral chambers to house the deceased's mummified body and the supplies, food, weapons, jewels, sacred pets, and furniture so the soul would be prepared for its next life.

❀ The Irish culture—steeped in myth and lore—celebrates the departed one's life with a "wake" prior to burial. With plenty of dancing and merrymaking they make a last-ditch effort to "wake up" the deceased and confuse evil spirits that might be lurking nearby.

❀ In Mexico and other Latin countries, the living celebrate their deceased relatives on El Día de los Muertos, or the Day of the Dead. This pre-Columbian custom celebrates death as the passage to a new life.

Thank-You Acknowledgments

If you are interested in printing your own acknowledgment cards, here are some examples of what the phrasing should look like with the words centered on the card. Remember to include a handwritten personal note of thanks, too.

The family of
(name of deceased)
acknowledges with deep appreciation your
kind expression of sympathy.

We will forever cherish the life of
(<u>name of deceased</u>)
and eternally wave to the heavens as (<u>he/she</u>)
begins (<u>his/her</u>) journey among the stars.
Our family sincerely thanks you for your
sympathy and thoughtfulness.

(<u>name of widow/widower/ family name</u>)
gratefully acknowledges your loving expression
of sympathy during this sorrowful time of mourning.

For Your Kindness and Sympathy—Thank You from the Heart—Sample Notes

Here are a few notes to help you show your friends and family
how much you appreciate their sympathy.

Thank You on Behalf of the Family

Dear _____,

*On behalf of my <u>(mother, father, grandmother, family)</u>,
please accept <u>(her/his/their)</u> sincere thanks for the <u>(card,
letter, flowers, food, financial contribution, or other gift)</u>
you sent in memory of <u>(name of deceased)</u>. It is only the
generosity of good friends like you that has gotten us through
this difficult time. Thank you.*

Respectfully yours,

_____

Thank You for Your Charitable Donation

Dear _____,

I know how much (name of deceased) treasured your friendship. If there was anyone in this world (he/she) loved and respected, it was you. Thank you for honoring (him/her) with your generous charitable donation to (name of charity). I am certain (he/she) would be so proud.

With my sincere appreciation,

_____

Thank You—Clergy

Dear _____,

This is definitely a moment in my life where I feel I am being tested by God. It seems so unfair for our loved ones to pass. While I am certain that (name of deceased) is in a better place, it has been so painful to say good-bye with grace and dignity. Thank you for helping me grieve, laugh, and cry. Thank you for showing me how to heal. God bless you.

Faithfully yours,

_____

GREATFUL SAGE TIP

Crane & Co. makes it easy to purchase personalized and generic sympathy acknowledgment cards, memorial cards, and stationery online.

⚮

Thanks for Your Expression of Sympathy

Dear_____,

*There are simply no words to thank you for the loving
expression of sympathy you have given us during the passing
of (name of deceased). We are so deeply grateful.*

With our love,

_____

Thank You for the Flowers or Funeral Wreath

Dear _____,

*Your love and support during this tremendously difficult time
is so greatly appreciated. The gorgeous white flowers you sent
were spectacular, and I know that (name of deceased)
would have loved them. On behalf of my family, I thank you.*

Gratefully yours,

_____

Thank You for the Food

Dear _____,

*I understand you are grieving just as deeply as we are. Please
know how much we appreciated the (food item) you brought
by. It was absolutely delicious and we know it was made with
all of your love. Thank you for taking the time to comfort us.*

Sincerely yours,

_____

Thank You for the Loving Tribute

Dear _____,

My (mother/father/other family member/name of deceased)
was the light of our life. Thank you for honoring (her/him)
with your loving tribute. We are forever grateful for the
heartwarming memories you have shared with us and we
will treasure them for a lifetime.

Love,

_____

Words have the power to both destroy and heal.
When words are both true and kind, they can change
our world.

—BUDDHA, ENLIGHTENED TEACHER

Index